New Product Development and Delivery

Ensuring Successful Products Through Integrated Process Management

Dale Brethauer

AMACOM

American Management Association

New York • Atlanta • Brussels • Buenos Aires • Chicago • London • Mexico City
San Francisco • Shanghai • Tokyo • Toronto • Washington, D.C.

Special discounts on bulk quantities of AMACOM books are available to corporations, professional associations, and other organizations. For details, contact Special Sales Department, AMACOM, a division of American Management Association, 1601 Broadway, New York, NY 10019.
Tel.: 212-903-8316. Fax: 212-903-8083.
Web site: www.amacombooks.org

This publication is designed to provide accurate and authoritative information in regard to the subject matter covered. It is sold with the understanding that the publisher is not engaged in rendering legal, accounting, or other professional service. If legal advice or other expert assistance is required, the services of a competent professional person should be sought.

Stage-Gate is a trademark of R.G. Cooper & Associates Consultants Inc. AMACOM uses Stage-Gate throughout this book for editorial purposes only, with no intention of trademark violation. R.G. Cooper & Associates Consultants Inc. should be contacted for complete information regarding trademarks and registration.

Library of Congress Cataloging-in-Publication Data

Brethauer, Dale M.
    New product development and delivery : ensuring successful products through integrated process management / Dale Brethauer.
        p.   cm.
    Includes index.
    ISBN 0-8144-0713-7
    1. New products—Marketing.   I. Title.

HF5415.153 .B74   2002
    658.8—dc21   2001045907

Printing number

10   9   8   7   6   5   4   3   2   1

I dedicate this book to my children:
Melissa, Kady, and Zachary.

Contents

Figures

Successfully launching new products is the lifeblood of most industries. Companies are looking for a steady stream of successful and profitable new products. The challenge is to identify the product ideas that actually have the most opportunity and then to coordinate the development of the product all the way from research and development (R&D) to the market launch.

New product development ranks among the riskiest and most confusing tasks for most companies. As the number of dollars invested in new product development goes up, the pressure to maximize the return on those investments also goes up. *New Product Development and Delivery* can help reduce the confusion of managing the new product development effort and increase the likelihood of successfully launching more new products.

This book teaches sixteen communication, task, and financial tools that set the groundwork for a successful product development and delivery process. It also includes a number of worksheets that will help any organization develop a structured process.

Chapter 6 essentially captures the process that my company, Proliant, Inc., went through when we set out to improve the way we developed new products.

A Proliant team, working with Dale Brethauer and using the concepts in this book, developed a very successful new product transfer process. We call our process PRIDE, which stands for PRoduct and Idea Development Excellence. The most visible benefit we gained after launching PRIDE was that we began to use a common language throughout the company. The once confusing conversation attempting to explain the status of a research project was replaced with a clear explanation of what stage the project was in and what tasks various people throughout the company were completing.

Each project now has a cross-functional team, allowing us to strategically place the people on each team who can deal with the many issues of a project as they arise. Perhaps more important is that PRIDE projects are considered a companywide effort and not just an R&D project.

Resources are limited, so efficient use of people, time, and money is the key to maximizing the return of new product development efforts. Using the Stage-Gate process described in this book has allowed us to more effectively allocate our resources to key projects and has, more importantly, given us the tools to terminate nonviable projects earlier.

The ultimate success of our new product process is its effect on Proliant's bottom line. We have increased the number of new products brought to market, and we do it in about half the cycle time as in the past. This did not happen overnight. It has required upper management support, a champion within the organization to drive the process, training, and the dedication of our technical people.

Managing the new product development effort requires planning, organization, discipline, and the passion of a cross-functional team working toward a market launch. Thank you, Dale, for helping us develop PRIDE and for providing us with the tools to develop our ideas into successful products.

Steve Welch
Vice President R&D
Proliant, Inc.

New Product Development and Delivery is a comprehensive guide for successfully transferring new products from R&D to manufacturing and market launch. It leads readers through 16 proven tools and techniques for new product transfer success and the development and implementation of a corporate transfer process.

The early chapters provide a detailed description of the tools and techniques. The later chapters discuss the development of a proven transfer process and the implementation of this process to gain buy-in within the corporation from the top to the bottom.

Successful transfer of new products through the organization is a common problem throughout industry. The writing of this book is timely. The successful implementation of a new product transfer process will make a company competitive into the future.

The United States is falling behind in the competitive-edge race. We have lost position in the smokestack industries (1970), appliances (1975), automotive (1980), electronics (1985), and new product development (1990).[1] The reason for this is not low-cost labor, modern equipment, product dumping, or copying products. It stems from an unprecedented race in all aspects of manufacturing: quality, machine technology, inventory turns, and new product launches. The time for new product launches has decreased from decades to months. New products have a direct effect on revenue generation, the number one reason for a company's staying competitive and reaching its goal of continually making money.

I thank Ray O'Connell, my editor at AMACOM, for his support and guidance with this project. I am a champion for this material. I am available for any questions or comments and may be reached at:

Dale Brethauer
Brethauer Consulting Group, Inc.
755 Beversrede Trail
Suite 1201
West Chester, PA 19382
(610) 388-3260
daleb@brethauerconsulting.com

The contents of this book are also taught at a two-day seminar. Schedules and additional information may be found at:

www.brethauerconsulting.com

NOTES

1. *The Goal,* by Eliyahu M. Goldratt (Great Barrington, Mass.: North River Press, 1986).

Chapter 1

The Foundation Elements of Successful Transfers

We have entered a period of new product launches unlike any other since the Industrial Revolution. Companies feel ever-increasing pressure to get new products to market faster. As new products are developed, successful new product transfer from research and development (R&D) to manufacturing is a common problem for companies of all sizes. Companies need to find ways to improve this new product transfer process and remain profitable and competitive.

In many companies, internal new product transfers are accomplished serially. That is, activities are completed in one department at a time and then passed on to the next department with little or no communication. Unfortunately, this idea has never worked very well (see Figure 1-1).

The best internal transfer process (1) integrates all departments at the same time into the process yielding a gap-free transfer, (2) builds on solid tools and techniques that streamline execution and produce effective results, and (3) is developed and implemented such that the whole company embraces the transfer process (see Figure 1-2).

Companies that learn to accelerate their new product launches by using a successful new product transfer process will enjoy these benefits:

- A competitive advantage

- The ability to be responsive to customers' needs

3

■ An increase in profitability

■ An increase in total quality

■ Decreased cycle time to bring a new product to market

■ A companywide feeling of accomplishment

■ A continuously improving company

Figure 1-1. A successful product transfer eliminates new product fumbles.

Artwork by Halus Haines.

Successful companies have both strategic goals and tactical programs to accomplish those goals. Strategic goals are set to keep a company competitive in the marketplace. For example, a company's strategic goals may be

Figure 1-2. Product transfer plan.

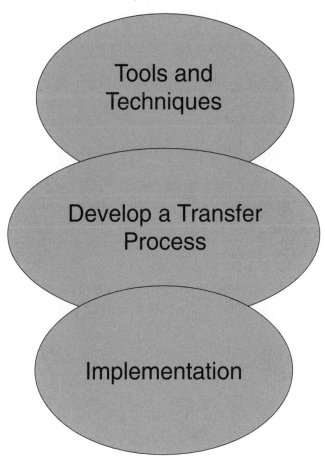

Tools and Techniques

Develop a Transfer Process

Implementation

to launch 40 new products and increase net profits by 10 percent. The tactical program to accomplish those goals would include a successful new product transfer process.

What does this mean for the bottom line? Statistics show that new product releases into the market (launched within five years) account for about 45 percent of an average company's annual revenues. This figure has risen 10 percent in just the past decade. However, only a scant 10 percent of all new products are successful in the market. Therefore, this 10 percent of a company's new product releases are responsible for almost half its annual revenue. That means that 90 percent of new products never produce revenue. One reason is that companies waste valuable time and money developing good products that never see the light of day because the company lacks an effective internal transfer process. Clearly, companies are dependent on their ability to transfer new products within the company successfully to ensure successful release into the market.

Let's look at a hypothetical example. ABC Co. has $500 million revenue and typically launches 25 to 50 new products each year. Therefore, its new product releases are generating about $240 million in annual revenue. If ABC Co. spends on average about 8 percent of sales on R&D, it is spending about $40 million per year on developing new products. If only an average of 10 percent of ABC's new products are successful, the organization should be working on about 500 new products in order to produce 50 successful ones. If ABC Co. increased its successful new product releases from 10 percent to 15 percent, it would have a potential increase in annual revenue of $100 million.

With such high stakes and potential for substantial increased revenue, it makes good business sense to implement a successful internal transfer process to accomplish the vital task of sustaining and improving your company's competitive advantage.

New product introductions are often treated as intru-

sions into a department's regular activities, so it's no sur-
prise that these introductions rarely go smoothly. It's even
rarer that they go quickly.

This book explains and illustrates a successful transfer
process and what it takes to implement one. Chapters 2
through 4 discuss the tools and techniques for successful
development and transfer of products from initial concept
through development, preproduction, production, and
market launch.

Seven keys to successful product transfer are:

■ Clear objectives

■ A cross-functional team approach

■ Upper management support

■ Customer-supplier involvement

■ Robust design and product

■ A structured process methodology

■ Economic justification

The seven keys may be organized into three groups:
communication tools, robust design and product tools,
and financial tools (see Figure 1-3).

I present 16 tools that will help any organization focus
on the activities necessary for success:

■ Clear objectives

　Tool 1: SMART Objectives

　Tool 2: Achieving Group Consensus

- A cross-functional team approach

  Tool 3: Selecting a Cross-Functional Team

  Tool 4: The Concept of a Champion

  Tool 5: Productive Meetings

- Upper management support

- Customer-supplier involvement

- Robust design and product

  Tool 6: Fit-for-Use/Deliverables Checklist

  Tool 7: Pareto's Law (Reduce Production Costs)

  Tool 8: Value-Added Flow Analysis

  Tool 9: Design for Manufacturing, Assembly, Experimentation, and Testing

- Structured process methodology

  Tool 10: Front-End Loading

  Tool 11: Stage-Gate Methodology

  Tool 12: Process Metrics

  Tool 13: Process Audit

- Economic justification

  Tool 14: Cost Estimating

  Tool 15: Economic Measures of Merit

  Tool 16: Setting Project Priorities

Figure 1-3. Seven keys to successful product transfer.

Communication Tools:

Clear objectives
Cross-functional team approach
Upper management support
Customer-supplier involvement

Robust Design and Product Tools:

Robust design and product
Structured process methodology

Financial Tools:

Economic justification

These tools are already widely used independent of each other within industry. Here, however, they are pulled together to help guide your product transfer plan.

In Chapters 5 and 6 you will learn how to develop a transfer process plan for your organization. We finish by discussing implementation of a process plan such that the whole company embraces the process.

Examples of successful processes and worksheets are provided to guide you and your company through the development of a process specific to your company's needs. They also include the success story of a medium-size company whose new product transfer process was developed over six months in 1998.

A transfer process is only as good as the paper it is printed on until it is implemented and embraced by the whole organization. These chapters illustrate the steps to implement the process in your company. You will be able to visualize how the total transfer process is developed and implemented from start to finish. Good luck on your journey!

Chapter 2

Communication Tools

Of the three areas of importance for the success of a transfer process, the most important by far is communication. Although this may seem obvious to most companies, very little effort is in fact put forth to improve communications. Establishing a cross-functional team (gathering workers from all major divisions or departments within the organization) is a good start but not the total answer. The team itself needs some tools to become efficient and effective and to excel in communication.

CLEAR OBJECTIVES

Teams fail for a number of reasons. The number one and number two reasons are unclear and changing objectives.[1] Other reasons are set out in Figure 2-1.

Figure 2-1. Why teams fail.

Goals unclear	55%
Changing objectives	55%
Lack of accountability	51%
Lack of management support	49%
Lack of role clarity	47%
Ineffective leadership	45%
Low priority of team	40%
No team-based pay	30%

Source: Hays Group

Michael Schrage, author of *No More Teams!* says, "Nobody wants to talk about the difficulties of moving millions of workers into the uncharted waters of teamwork. It's just not that easy. Anyone who's ever been on a team knows that."[2] To combat this attitude, many companies are finding that new product transfer teams start more smoothly and stay on track better if their first task is developing their objectives or criteria for success of the new product.

Tool 1: SMART Objectives

Setting objectives is the first task of the new product development team. Those objectives then become the criteria by which the team developing the product will be judged. There are some major advantages of developing objectives as the first team task:

- Total team buy-in becomes a by-product as all individuals work on the development of project objectives.

- The purpose of the team and its mission becomes clearer.

- Hidden agendas become defused as team members reach agreement on the objectives.

Reaching consensus on the criteria of success is an important aspect of team building. As the team evolves, objectives may be modified, but they will always stand out as the guiding light and direction for the process. Always save the first objective statement. If a change in direction is made, the original objective may be modified. This ever-green objective will also help explain changes in direction from the original objective.

There are many ways to help a team develop objectives, but the best method is referred to as establishing SMART objectives. It is successfully practiced by many organizations today. In order for a team's objectives to be SMART objectives, they must be:

Specific

Measurable

Achievable

Realistic

Time specific

When these five elements are stated in an objective statement, all criteria for success are spelled out.

Following are some examples of SMART and non-SMART objectives. See for yourself if the SMART objective illuminates the path:

Non-SMART objective: "The product must be reliable."

SMART objective: "The new surveillance camera must perform 24 hours per day with only 2 percent downtime. This new enhancement must be released by the fourth quarter this year."

Consider how the second statement of objectives meets all the criteria for a SMART objective:

Specific	"new [surveillance camera] enhancement"
Measurable	"2 percent downtime"
Achievable	"must perform"
Realistic	Is 2 percent downtime realistic?
Time specific	"by the fourth quarter this year"

Here is another example:

Non-SMART objective: "Training will be completed by the fourth quarter."

SMART objective: "Training for all personnel will be completed according to the developed document for product transfer by December 15 of this year."

Once again, consider how the second statement of objectives meets all the criteria for a SMART objective:

Specific	"training . . . for product transfer"
Measurable	"for all personnel"
Achievable	"will be completed"
Realistic	"training for all"
Time specific	"by December 15 of this year"

Establishing SMART objectives early in the life of the project also sets out the framework so that the team members will know when they have accomplished the task. Because the members of the team had to agree on the elements of the objective, they own the responsibility for the project, thus gaining buy-in by all before proceeding.

Tool 2: Achieving Group Consensus

Consensus is a state of mutual agreement among members of a group where all concerns of individuals have been addressed and answered to the satisfaction of the group. Here are the main reasons for seeking group consensus:

- It ensures member commitment to the ultimate decisions.

- A win-win attitude replaces the win-lose mentality of the voting method.

- It raises the quality of decision making, reduces errors, and contributes to group synergy.

- It increases the group's willingness to take responsibility for outcomes.

The following story shows the power of group consensus. In eight years of teaching seminars with the American Management Association, I have used a weighted average technique to reach a consensus decision. I have asked hundreds of groups to estimate the current value of gold in dollars per troy ounce. I ask everyone to write their guess on a small piece of paper and assess their expertise. Those who rate their expertise as nonexistent are in expertise level 1. Anybody with even a slight knowledge is in expertise level 2. Anyone who has noticed the price of gold in the paper within a year or is an active trader is in expertise level 3.

I then collect the pieces of paper and write the answers on a flip chart, dividing the information into three columns—one for each expertise level. I total each column, then multiply column 1 total by one, column 2 total by two, and column 3 total by three. This method gives the most weight to the guesses in group 3—the people with the most expertise. The three columns are then totaled and divided by the number of guesses made. The final number is the group's estimate of the current price of gold. In the eight years that I have been running this exercise, the estimates have varied but never further from the actual current price than 10 percent. This technique shows the power of a weighted-average consensus estimate. Figure 2-2 shows a recent consensus decision on the price of gold from a group of 17 people who were attending one of my classes.

Figure 2-2. Weighted average consensus on the price of gold.

Group 1		Group 2		Group 3
$35.00		$320.00		$310.00
$100.00		$375.00		$305.00
$200.00		$325.00		$308.00
$1.50		$400.00		$305.00
$50.00		$250.00		
$400.00		$300.00		
		$400.00		
$786.50		$2,370.00		$1,228.00
x 1		x 2		x 3
$786.50		$4,740.00		$3,684.00

Add the three columns in Figure 2-2:

$786.50
4,740.00
3,684.00
$9,210.50

Then add the total number of guesses:

Column 1:   6 × 1   =   6
Column 2:   7 × 2   =   14
Column 3:   4 × 3   =   12
                         32

The estimate for the current price of gold would be:

$9,210.50 ÷ 32 = $288

On November 12, 1997, when this estimate was made, the price of gold was $307. This group came within $19 of the actual price, or an estimate within 6 percent. I'd call that a good estimate.

CROSS-FUNCTIONAL TEAM APPROACH

Working in teams has primary benefits in the following areas:

- *Communications.* Team members realize how important it is to pass on information.

- *Collaboration.* Individuals willingly invest themselves in the team effort.

- *Resources.* Whenever one member of the team lacks knowledge or competence, another is there to fill the gap.

- *Decisions.* Decisions are made more quickly because individuals make their choices together.

- *Commitment.* Individuals who are responsible for decisions own them.

- *Quality.* Members naturally want their team to achieve quality and accuracy, and therefore succeed.

People need information and feedback to bring about and manage change effectively. If the transfer process uses a team approach, it can have a major positive impact on the productivity, performance, and potential of the new product development. However, a team cannot just be thrown together and be expected to perform. Selecting the team's members with care can greatly improve the process.

Tool 3: Selecting a Cross-Functional Team

The successful transfer of products through the organization depends on the output of a cross-functional and diverse team rather than the efforts of individuals or a homogeneous group.

A cross-functional team includes key members from each division or department involved in a new product transfer—typically R&D, engineering, manufacturing, and marketing. (You should determine your company's critical divisions in addition to these four and include members from those divisions on a core team.) Communications will be greatly improved if manufacturing and marketing personnel are involved early in the new product development effort. Their work will help guide a smoother transition as the product development proceeds.

A diverse team will also increase the team's overall effectiveness. When people are blended together with different backgrounds, different knowledge bases, different preferences, and different likes and dislikes, a more productive team emerges. For example, teams having all members who are detail-oriented will surely miss the big picture. Similarly, a team of only analytical people might miss the true product value because the data tell them differently.

How does a company then choose a diverse group for their transfer team? The work of Carl Jung proves to be extremely useful here. From his discussions with patients and clients in his psychoanalytical and psychiatric work, Jung identified different life orientations:

Extroversion and Introversion—describing how people prefer to relate with others

Sensing and Intuition—explaining how people prefer to relate to their world

Thinking and Feeling—defining how people prefer to interpret their world

Isabel Briggs Myers later developed and extended these concepts to include the Judging and Perceiving dimension on how people respond to their world.[3] Later still, Margerison and McCann developed the Team Management Index, a modification of the Myers-Briggs instrument specifically aimed at the work environment and preferences.[4] Their model used four categories:

- How people prefer to relate with others

- How people prefer to gather and use information

- How people prefer to make decisions

- How people prefer to organize themselves and others

Each day at work, we have to relate to others in order to get work done. Some people do this in an extroverted way, meeting frequently with others, talking through ideas, and enjoying a variety of tasks and activities. Other people are more introverted, preferring to think things through on their own before speaking and generally not having much daily interaction with others. Teams need both types, or members may end up with everyone talking and expressing themselves without some essential deep thinking going on. On the other hand, if everyone just sat around and thought without expressing themselves, no one would ever know where the others stood on an issue. Therefore, a balance of the two preferences is necessary to make an effective team.

As we relate to others, we gather and share information in either a practical or a creative way. Practical people prefer to work with tested ideas and pay attention to the facts and details, whereas creative people are more future-oriented, always looking for the possibilities in a situation.

For new product development, the creative personality is paramount; however, if left unchecked, the creative members might continue to optimize and modify a product with no concern about the ultimate product launch. On the other hand, a purely practical person might be so focused on what has been proven in the past that he or she might miss a truly unique chance to create a novel product. Here again a balance of the two preferences is necessary.

Once the team has gathered the information, it is necessary to make decisions. Some people go about this in an analytical way, setting up objective decision-making criteria and choosing the solution that maximizes benefits. Others tend to make decisions more according to their beliefs. Since nobody on the team will have a crystal ball to tell the future, decisions must be made on both the facts and a gut sense.

Finally, decisions have to be acted on. Some people like a structured environment where things are neat and tidy and always handled in the same manner. Others prefer to be more flexible, allowing for variances in a process. Although I advocate a structured new product transfer process, flexibility allows for conditions that might vary from the norm.

The four work preference types are summarized here:

- How people relate with others at work: Extroversion (E) and Introversion (I)

- How people wish to approach tasks by gathering and using information: Practical (P) and Creative (C) preferences

■ How people wish to make decisions: Analytical (A) and Beliefs (B) orientation

■ How people wish to organize themselves and others: Structured (S) or Flexible (F) approaches

Most individuals are not 100 percent of one type and 0 percent of the other but rather a mixture of both. I prefer to be an extrovert (E), creative (C), analytical (A), and structured (S)—an ECAS.

By using this tool, a company can put together a unique and extremely productive cross-functional and diverse work team. The following case study shows how a company might put this into practice.

Case Study: Wylie Fabricator

Wylie Fabricator was preparing to develop a new sheet material fabrication device. The original concept had been proposed to management, which saw the potential in such a device. In order to form a cross-functional team, management requested that everyone in the company do a work preference self-analysis and report their four-letter preference to their immediate supervisor. The breakdown by division and work preference type for Wylie's 16 employees is shown in Figure 2-3. Wylie has six divisions: R&D, Marketing, Manufacturing, Purchasing, Computer Services, and Engineering. The team will have four members, one from each of the four main divisions: R&D, Marketing, Manufacturing, and Engineering.

Management decides that the key person to the success of this development is the creator of the device, Sue, in Research and

Figure 2-3. Work preference chart for Wylie employees.

Employee	Division	Work Preference Profile
Mike	R&D	ICAF
Sue	R&D	ICBS
Jeff	R&D	ECAF
Bill	R&D	ICAF
Bridgette	Marketing	EPBF
James	Marketing	ECAF
Melissa	Marketing	EPBS
Dale	Manufacturing	ECAS
Steve	Manufacturing	ICAS
Joe	Manufacturing	ICAS
John	Manufacturing	ICAF
Brenda	Purchasing	EPBF
Carol	Computer Services	IPBS
Bill	Engineering	EPAF
Kim	Engineering	EPBF
Frank	Engineering	IPAS

Development. Her profile is ICBS. Because Sue has Introvert preferences, it is important to choose a person from another division with an Extrovert tendency. This could be Bridgette, James, or Melissa from Marketing, Dale from Manufacturing, or Kim from Engineering. The choice is Bridgette (EPBF) from Marketing, who has a profile almost exactly opposite to Sue's.

Two of the four critical divisions are now represented on the team. These two also provide a good balance of Introvert and Extrovert and Creative and Practical. Now, we need an analytical person to balance Bridgette's and Sue's belief preferences. John from Manufacturing, who has a profile of ICAF, is chosen. The team now has a member from each division except Engineering and has a good balance of preferences.

If it were possible to pick a person from Engineering with an EPAS profile, the team would have a perfect balance of work preferences. However, there are no profiles like that in Engineering, so the closest would be Bill or Frank. Management selects Bill because he has worked well with Sue on an earlier project. The cross-functional team for the sheet metal device is shown in Figure 2-4.

Figure 2-4. Wylie's cross-functional team for devices.

Employee	Division	Work Preference Profile
Sue	R&D	ICBS
Bridgette	Marketing	EPBF
John	Manufacturing	ICAF
Bill	Engineering	EPAF

Tool 4: The Concept of a Champion

A champion is someone who:

■ Is passionate about the product or idea

■ Has a clear vision

■ Wants to succeed beyond all expectations

■ Feels accountable

Some examples of successful champions who show all of these attributes are Art Frey with his invention and development of the 3M Post-it Notes™ and the Xerox team of Peter Warter, Jack Lewis, and Bruce Barton for their successful development of the Xerox 9700™ laser printer.

A champion can play a key role in the development of new products—for example:

- Initiating the transfer process

- Evaluating proposals for strategic importance

- Choosing core team members

- Preparing original back-of-the-envelope financial calculations

- Initiating the business plan for a product

- Providing vision in meetings

- Acting as a liaison between interested parties

The importance of this role cannot be overemphasized in the success of a new product transfer process.

Tool 5: Productive Meetings

When a great transfer process is developed, one of the biggest criticisms and sometimes the hardest hurdle to overcome during implementation is the perception that the process will be adding bureaucracy to the company. If cross-functional teams are added for each product being transferred, how will team members deal with all the necessary meetings?

If the transfer process requires better communications—through team meetings—then a tool to make meetings more productive will result in a more efficient process. One of the finest books written on the subject of productive meetings is Thomas Kayser's *Mining Group Gold*.[5]

More productive meetings may be accomplished through seven steps that provide better meeting planning and execution:

Planning

Step 1: Define the meeting purpose.

Step 2: Decide who should attend the meeting.

Step 3: Set the meeting agenda.

Execution

Step 4: Identify a facilitator.

Step 5: Identify a timekeeper.

Step 6: Identify a scribe.

Meeting Length

Step 7: Set the meeting length at a maximum of one hour.

Planning

"Efficient and productive meetings don't just happen. Because group sessions produce results that cannot be accomplished in any other way, careful planning of the meeting structure is a must. A clear understanding of what is to be accomplished is the foundation on which the entire session rests."[6]

In Step 1, the person who calls the meeting—if this is a regularly scheduled team meeting, it will be the team leader—must communicate the meeting purpose well in advance to allow the participants time to prepare. E-mail is an ideal medium to relay the purpose to all team participants. Each participant then has the responsibility to prepare for the meeting and/or feed back any discrepancies to the leader.

The leader must decide who is necessary at the meeting (Step 2). In order for the meeting to be efficient, the situation in which someone sits through a one-hour meeting and is necessary for only five minutes of it must be eliminated. A rule of thumb is to invite the fewest number of people required to achieve the desired outcome.

Along with communicating the purpose of the meeting, the leader must set the agenda (Step 3), with times allotted for each topic, and communicate the agenda in advance of the meeting. "Research has shown the group sessions with a clear-cut agenda tend to be better focused, significantly more effective, and achieve more specific results than meetings without an agenda."[7] A typical agenda may be seen in Figure 2-5.

Figure 2-5. Sample meeting agenda.

Agenda for APEX meeting, Jan. 7, 200x
8:30–9:30
Conference Room N6436A

10 minutes	Review results of the last meeting
30 minutes	Discuss technical aspects of the Bio program
10 minutes	Review schedule for January
5 minutes	Personnel conflicts

The three steps of defining the purpose, deciding who should attend, and setting the agenda set the stage for an efficient meeting.

Execution

The meeting execution requires identifying three key people in Steps 4 through 6: a facilitator, a timekeeper, and a scribe.

The facilitator, who may or may not be the leader, focuses on the meeting dynamics. In addition, the facilitator:

- Monitors the behavior of the group to minimize disruptions and keep the team focused.

- Quickly alerts the team when they are going off on a tangent.

- Helps the team identify when they seem to be going nowhere.

"The timekeeper monitors how long the team is taking to accomplish its tasks and provides regular updates to make members aware of where they are in regards to time spent."[8] It is, however, the facilitator's role to make sure the team stays within the time limits set on the agenda. Moving forward without a decision because the meeting has gone past the time limit is not allowed.

The scribe captures what is being said by team members, without censoring the remarks. The job of recording is done on a whiteboard or flip chart in front of the team for all to see. Meeting minutes may then be extracted from the scribe's notes after the conclusion of the meeting and sent to all participants.

Meeting Length

The last step is probably the most important: meetings should last only one hour. People generally can remain attentive to a topic for 20 minutes at most. A meeting lasting over one hour is really pushing it and can become unproductive. People are busy and appreciate a well-organized, well-run meeting that lasts only one hour. Two one-hour meetings are much more productive than one two-hour meeting.

UPPER MANAGEMENT SUPPORT

The successful development and implementation of a new product transfer process typically require substantial change within a company and therefore must be supported from the top. Companies with successful transfer processes enjoy ongoing visible support from top corporate levels. This does not mean that the process must be developed and run by upper management. Quite the contrary is the case. Once upper management has been informed and its concerns and comments about the process addressed, too much upper management involvement is likely to be counterproductive. This process works best if the day-to-day decisions are not made at the top of the organization. The emphasis is upper management support, not involvement.

CUSTOMER-SUPPLIER INVOLVEMENT

Companies have long recognized that success requires getting close to customers and suppliers. Only by better serving customer needs and making sure that new products meet those needs can companies be superior to their competitors. Also, as a new product moves through the development cycle, close communication with suppliers will ensure that essential materials can and will be available and delivered.

Close collaboration with customers and suppliers can produce dramatic results: higher margins, lower costs, more value for customers, and larger market share. Underlying such benefits are more specific gains:

- Ongoing cost reductions

- Quality improvements

- Shorter development cycle time

- Increased operating flexibility

- More powerful competitive strategies

NOTES

1. Ellen Neuborne, "Why Teams Fail," *USA Today,* Feb. 25, 1997.

2. Michael Schrage, *No More Teams!* (New York: Currency/Doubleday, 1995).

3. Otto Kroeger and Janet M. Thuesen, *Type Talk* (Dell Publishing, 1988), based on Myers-Briggs Type Indicator™.

4. Charles Margerison and Dick McCann, *Team Management Systems* (Prado Systems Limited, 1993)

5. Thomas A. Kayser, *Mining Group Gold* (Chicago, Irwin Professional Publishing, 1995). Kayser is the manager of organization effectiveness for the Office Document Systems Division of the Xerox Company.

6. Ibid.

7. Ibid.

8. Ibid.

Chapter 3

Robust Design and Product Tools

A company entering the marketplace with a new product has a marked advantage over the competition. However, unless precautions have been taken to keep competitors from copying the product, that advantage will soon deteriorate.

ROBUST DESIGN AND PRODUCT

Beginning at the early phases of product development and using the following tools and techniques that maximize quality, productivity, yields, and profitability will protect against the erosion:

- Tool 6: Fit-for-Use/Deliverables Checklist

- Tool 7: Pareto's Law (Reduce Production Costs)

- Tool 8: Value-Added Flow Analysis

- Tool 9: Design for Manufacturing, Assembly, Experimentation, and Testing

Tool 6: Fit-for-Use/Deliverables Checklist

A "fit-for-use" checklist will ensure that every item on the checklist is being considered as the project proceeds. These are the items that are necessary for a successful product launch and must be completed before the product is ready for sale. This checklist may also be used to identify items to be completed at different stages of the project before passing through to the next stage—for example:

"Meets customer expectations."

"The product and process are safe."

"The product meets the performance specifications."

"Sales and distribution channels are in place."

"The product meets regulatory requirements."

"Patent inquiry and search are completed."

Take some time now and develop a fit-for-use checklist for a project with which you have recently been associated. This checklist should be generic and useful to your future projects.

Tool 7: Pareto's Law (Reduce Production Costs)

In 1897, an Italian economist named Pareto discovered that the incomes of individuals were distributed by what has become known as the 80-20 rule: 80 percent of the money within an economic system is held by 20 percent of the people. When applied to the production process, this law quickly illuminates the areas to focus on when trying to reduce production costs. Of course, the distribution will not always be 80-20; nevertheless, it makes sense to focus on the big areas of cost first when trying for reductions. Look at the breakdown of the conversion costs associated with each area of the carpet manufacturing process shown in Figure 3-1. Using Pareto's law, which area would be the first one to focus on for cost-reduction efforts?

Figure 3-1. Cost breakdown for carpet manufacturing.

Area	Conversion Costs (dollars per square yard)
Twisting	.19
Heat set	.25
Tufting	.06
Dyeing	.05
Finishing	.06
Warehousing	.09
Total	.70

Tool 8: Value-Added Flow Analysis

To reduce costs and also improve quality, a company may use value-added flow analysis. Shortening the duration of a process is not about time management or just-in-time strategies. It is about eliminating the time that is spent on a product doing something that in the eyes of the customer would have no value. By eliminating some of those non-value-added steps, Rath and Strong, a management consulting firm headquartered in Lexington, Massachusetts, has proved that up to 75 percent of the time can be eliminated from any business process.[1]

The first step in the analysis is to block out a process step by step just as if the product were proceeding through the manufacturing activities. The second step is to write down the time it stays in each step. And the last is to determine whether the step adds value to the product. Edward J. Hay, senior vice president with Rath and Strong, suggests three rules to determine if a process step is value added:

1. The customer cares about it.

2. It physically changes the product.

3. It is done right the first time.[2]

This is relatively easy to do. I have found that the best people to do this analysis are the team members working with the operators who are producing the product. The analysis points out which steps could be eliminated. The hard part of value-added flow analysis is modifying or improving the process, through engineering, to eliminate those steps. Figure 3-2 shows a worksheet for performing a value-added flow analysis.

Let's look at an example using the production of the feedstock for carpets: twisted and heat set yarn. Figure 3-3 shows the 13 steps in the process. Notice, however, that only 2 steps are considered value adding and the time involved with those two steps is only a small fraction of the total time the product spends in production.

If a company focuses only on maintaining the two steps considered value adding, the process may be streamlined and costs reduced.

Tool 9: Design for Manufacturing, Assembly, Experimentation, and Testing

Design for manufacturing and design for assembly are extensions of the value analysis. In design for manufactur-

Figure 3-2. Value-added flow analysis worksheet.

No.	Activity	Time	Value-Added

Figure 3-3. Value-added steps for carpet yarns.

No.	Activity	Time	Value-Added
1	Transfer yarn from supplier	5 days	
2	Store yarn in warehouse	30 days	
3	Creel yarn packages for twisting	4 hours	
4	Twist yarn	1 hour	V
5	Doff packages of twisted yarn	1/4 hour	
6	Store twisted yarn in warehouse	30 days	
7	Ship to heat setter	5 days	
8	Store yarn in warehouse	30 days	
9	Creel yarn for heat setting	4 hours	
10	Heat set yarn in stuffer jet	1 hour	V
11	Doff package of twisted/heat set yarn	1/4 hour	
12	Store heat set yarn in warehouse	30 days	
13	Ship to tufter	5 days	

ing (DFM), we look for the optimum method of manufacturing a product in the most consistent and most reliable way, at minimum cost. In design for assembly (DFA), we look for the fewest number of assembly steps needed to put the product together, again at minimum cost.

Using Pareto's law, a company is able to identify the manufacturing steps that are the most costly. Then, using value-added flow analysis, the only important value-added steps are identified. Now, using DFM and DFA, the company can focus on the engineering of the manufacturing process.

Typically, a product is designed and detailed and a prototype manufactured before a cost estimate is attempted. That is too late. The opportunity to consider radically different products and process structures has been lost, and among the alternatives might have been a version that is substantially less expensive to produce. Thus, a conflict exists. On the one hand, the designer needs cost estimates as a basis for making sound decisions and seeing the effect that DFM and DFA are having on cost. On the other hand, the product design is not sufficiently firm to allow accurate estimates to be made using currently available techniques. The means of overcoming this dilemma are covered under Tool 14: Cost Estimating.

"Doing DFM and DFA without a cross-functional team is inviting failure," says Paula M. Noaker. She continues, "Storage Technology, Inc. is now in its seventh year of a corporatewide effort to convert all projects to a formal transfer process including cross-functional teams and DFM. To foster the cross-functional team concept and breakdown the traditional us versus them mindset, the firm redirected its career path for R&D and manufacturing personnel. R&D personnel, for instance, often follow a project into production, transferring back after market launch."[3]

Design of experimentation (DOE) is another tool that can be used for problem solving, process improvement, or understanding the underlying mechanisms of the manufacturing process. DOE has been credited with seemingly magical improvements in cost, quality, and productivity. Figure 3-4 depicts the three major steps in DOE:

1. Define the problem.

2. Identify the major *factors* affecting outputs.

3. Conduct an analysis that identifies how to squeeze the most from *responses.*

Figure 3-4. Design of experimentation steps.

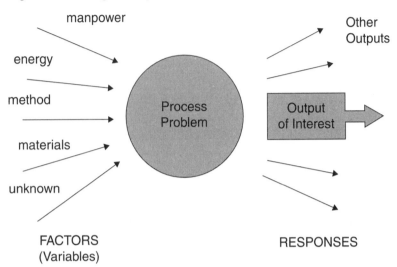

In the example in Figure 3-5, time, pressure, and temperature are the key independent variables, and quality and improved strength are the measurable responses.

Figure 3-5. Example design of experimentation variables and responses.

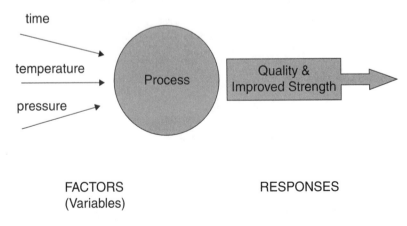

There are 11 common types of DOE schemes. The one I like the best is called *Box-Behken.*

If an experimenter was running an experiment with three variables at Levels 2, 3, and 5, as shown in Figure 3-6, to get all the outputs would require that 30 experiments be run: $(2 \times 3 \times 5) = 30$. This is called a *full factorial DOE.* The number of experiments needed is the factorial calculation.

Figure 3-6. Full factorial design of experimentation.

Full Factorial—consists of every possible combination of the factors and levels chosen for the experiment. Usually used with few factors.

Factors	Level
1	2
2	3
3	5

$(2 \times 3 \times 5) = 30$ tests

With the Box-Behken approach to experimentation, the number of tests necessary is reduced considerably. It was specifically created for use with factors set at three levels, as seen in Figure 3-7.

Using the setup described in Figure 3-7, an experimenter can test every combination of the two factors while holding the other variable at its center position. Therefore, there are only nine tests necessary to get all the output data required. The output data may then be displayed on a contour plot, as shown in Figure 3-8, which shows time versus temperature and the resulting output from the responses. The contour plot looks similar to a topographical map. If the experimenter were looking for

Figure 3-7. Box-Behken approach to design of experimentation.

Box-Behken—created specifically for use with factors set at
three levels.

Factors	Level
1	3
2	3
3	1

(3 x 3 x 1) = 9 tests

the highest value (improved strength), then he or she would set time at 1 and temperature at 3 to give the highest value possible.

Another tool, design for testing (DFT), is necessary for many companies. Sometimes it is not possible to design and develop a product without first specifying the test method, test points, and even an automated testing system for the product. Sometimes specific test instruments must be purchased for customer validation. The product design and process flow must accommodate these specific instruments. If testing can be automated and fed back to the process control room, corrections are made automatically online, and tight quality standards may be maintained. Statistical quality control within 6 sigma is possible (3.14 ppm reject). These testing systems are an integral part of any transfer process. Development of the test system is an effort that is parallel to DFM, DFA, and DOE.

Figure 3-8. Contour plot.

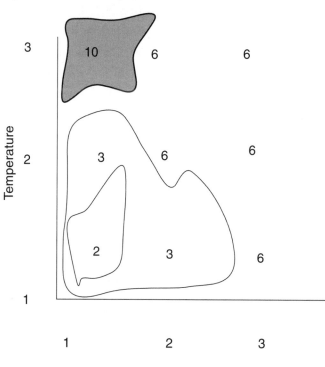

STRUCTURED PROCESS METHODOLOGY

Tools 6–9 help in the development of a robust product. The next four tools (front-end loading, Stage-Gate methodology, process metrics, and process audit) focus on developing a robust transfer process.

Tool 10: Front-End Loading

The time to use high levels of manpower resources on a project to compare a variety of alternatives is during the first phases of the project. This is commonly referred to as front-end loading. The graph in Figure 3-9 shows that the exposure to financial risk is relatively low in the early stages of a project but rapidly increases as the project proceeds though development. The financial risk is largest during the commercialization phase, when major investments are made. Therefore, it makes good sense to see that the process is optimized before entering the later, more costly phases of the project.

Figure 3-9. Front-end loading.

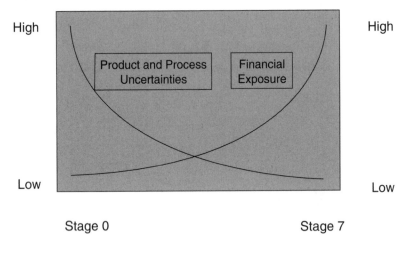

The project team should check out as many alternative solutions as possible. One technique to use for determining different solutions is brainstorming. By using the following technique, a team may diverge on a wide variety of possible solutions and then converge on the most promising:

Brainstorming Technique

1. The team leader presents the problem.

2. All members sketch their solution on an overhead transparency.

3. Each member has five minutes to present his or her idea.

4. The whole group votes on their favorite solution.

5. The team evaluates the consensus solution.

The brainstorming process usually starts with the transfer team's convening a large group (15 to 20 people works well) with some familiarity with the new product. A member of the transfer team presents the new product or idea and the problem it is being developed to solve. Then everyone in the larger group is asked to come up with ideas to solve the problem and make a sketch to present on an overhead transparency. Allow about 15 minutes to create solutions.

The ideas are presented one at a time by each member of the group. After each idea is presented, it is displayed on the room wall. No negative comments are allowed during the presentation; only clarification questions are allowed. If there are 20 people in the group, the presentation phase will take a little over an hour and a half.

Once all of the ideas are presented, the floor may be open for discussion. Everyone in the group is given five sticky dots and asked to vote for their top five ideas by placing the dot on the displayed transparencies. Through this process, the group's ideas will converge into a few that should be analyzed and evaluated as potential solutions.

Tool 11: Stage-Gate Methodology

A game plan or road map for product development through commercialization is a necessary tool to plan, manage, direct, and control new product efforts. The Stage-Gate model in Tool 11 incorporates many of the other tools already discussed, as well as tools discussed later in this book. Using the Stage-Gate model will heighten the effectiveness of the transfer process in the following ways:

- Focusing on the completeness of all tasks necessary for a successful product launch

- Focusing on quality of execution

- Helping to prioritize projects through constant financial analysis

- Requiring a cross-functional team approach

- Shortening the time to product launch by allowing tasks to be performed in parallel

- Involving the customer and supplier throughout development

- Forcing the exploration of alternative approaches early in new product development

- Reducing risk

The Stage-Gate methodology also structures an operational model for moving a new product from idea to launch. A structured, consistent approach to development helps an organization rapidly initiate an effort and drive to a logical end point through a series of stages and gates. This approach increases efficiency and reduces cycle time by standardizing repeatable stages and tasks from one project to the next. Moreover, the audit of the process allows individuals to learn from the experiences of previous projects that have used the Stage-Gate process. A structured Stage-Gate process is a uniform methodology tailored to the needs of an individual project. It therefore leads to a common understanding of the stages and tasks within each stage, the implementation procedures, and the responsibilities. Among its benefits are more effective teamwork across functional lines, problem resolution early in the life of the process, and improved communication.

Robert Gravlin Cooper has called the Stage-Gate system "a blueprint for managing the new product process to improve effectiveness and efficiency. Stage-Gate™ systems break the innovation process into a predetermined set of stages, each stage consisting of a set of prescribed, multifunctional, and parallel activities. The entrance to each stage is a gate: gates control the process and serve as the quality control and Go/Kill checkpoints. This 'stage-and-gate' format leads to the name 'Stage-Gate system.'"[4]

A typical Stage-Gate process is shown in Figure 3-10 and detailed below.

Stage 0: Idea concept. An idea is reviewed with management, which assesses the strategic fit, business merit, and

Figure 3-10. Stage-Gate process.

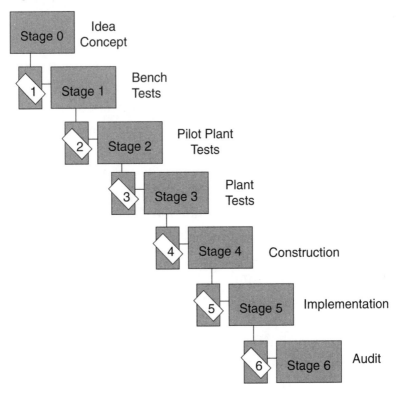

technical feasibility of the new idea. If the idea merits attention, a cross-functional team for carrying out the project is
put together. The team begins to explore alternative technical solutions and put together initial project specifications
along with preliminary economics. The idea or product
concept is refined, and the target market is identified.

Stage 1: Bench tests. Product lab samples are prepared,
and the product definition and optimization at the bench
scale are completed.

Stage 2: Pilot plant tests. Pilot plant samples are made, and the product definition is tightened. The product samples made are tested internally through alpha testing (internal testing). The environmental impacts are assessed.

Stage 3: Plant tests. During this stage the product is produced using the exact process steps identified for production. The product should be identical to the final marketed product. At the end of this stage, one of the most important, the team reviews with management its progress on the product in preparation for beginning the construction of the facility or modification to an existing process. After this stage, the costs of the project begin to escalate at a rapid rate.

Stage 4: Construction. This stage has only one task: constructing and installing a facility if necessary for the production of the new product.

Stage 5: Implementation. The first production run takes place, followed by debugging of the process. The market launch is planned and executed.

Stage 6: Audit. The project is audited and the metrics tallied. This is a very important stage for the continuous improvement of the company. (The process metrics and audit are Tools 12 and 13.)

Each stage is designed to gather information needed for the project to progress through the next gate review. Each stage consists of varying tasks to be performed by various divisions within the company. The task activities are designed to gather information about the product and decrease the uncertainties.

The stages are further divided into major tasks that fulfill the requirements of each stage. The specific activities within each task are defined by the cross-functional team based on the unique needs of each project.

After completion of a stage and before passing through to the next stage, a review should be held in which major project decisions will be made, whether to proceed to the tasks in the next stage, redirect efforts within the current stage, or kill the project. This compartmentalization of a project reduces the risk of proceeding too far with a project that instead should be stopped. Also, as the project passes through the stages, the cost to the company increases. The Stage-Gate process allows for an incremental cost commitment by the company.

Gate reviews are a critical element in the development Stage-Gate methodology. During these reviews, management makes strategic decisions, allocates personnel, provides physical and financial resources, and gives direction and leadership to the project team. These reviews should differ from technical reviews and should focus more on the project's business and strategic issues. The gate reviews are not intended to take the place of technical reviews, project status reviews, or presentations. These should still be held when needed.

Robert Gravlin Cooper has provided some success stories as a result of using Stage-Gate methodology:[5]

■ After a rather dismal track record for new products and models throughout the 1980s, General Motors moved to fast-paced innovation. It developed and then implemented its copyrighted four-phase system, essentially a Stage-Gate system, for product design and introduction, which has already drastically cut the concept-to-launch time of a new car model.

■ 3M has an enviable new product track record. An innovative corporate culture and climate are often cited as 3M's secret to success, but for years 3M has had in place various Stage-Gate systems for managing the innovation process. Thus, creativity and discipline are blended to yield a successful new product program.

■ Procter & Gamble has recently faced tougher times in its new product efforts. One recommendation of a senior management task force was to "get back to basics and redesign and reimplement the Stage-Gate process." In 1991, P&G relaunched a 1990s version of its game plan: a six-stage model, or "product launch road map," for driving new products to market.

Among other companies that have implemented new product game plans or Stage-Gate systems are Northern Telecom, Corning, Exxon Chemicals, Hewlett-Packard, Ethyl Corporation, and various divisions at DuPont, Emerson Electric, and B. F. Goodrich.

Tool 12: Process Metrics

Process metrics is used to monitor the transfer process and its effectiveness in creating positive change in product development activities. Metrics also provides tools for diagnosing deficiencies in the transfer process and accelerating new learnings about continuous improvement. The metrics should be directly tied to the goals of the transfer process. All companies will develop their own metrics. Following are some sample metrics for specified goals:

Goal: Reduce cycle time.

Metric: Actual versus forecast cycle times.

Definition: Months required moving through all the stages and months required completing each stage versus forecast.

Purpose: To build a database to determine how actual cycle time performance compares to expectations. Attention should be paid not only to noting the actual cycle times, but also to relating the cycle times to factors such as team experience, project urgency, project delays, and project complexity.

Goal: Increase the probability that projects will be successful.

Metric: Number of successful projects.

Definition: Total number of projects completed versus total number started.

Purpose: To determine the number of successful projects.

Goal: Develop more products and ideas company-wide.

Metric: Number of new product launches per year.

Definition: A list of all transfer projects and new product launches.

Purpose: To monitor the use and effectiveness of the formal transfer process.

Goal: Develop management commitment to the transfer process.

Metric: Resources provided.

Definition: Management is providing the necessary resources—both people and funding.

Purpose: To determine if the process is getting proper management support.

Goal: Develop a more user-friendly process.

Metric: Positive reaction to the process by the team after a project has been completed.

Definition: A positive vote.

Purpose: To determine if the team still buys into the transfer process's effectiveness.

Goal: Market recognition of the process.

Metric: Number of transfer process references.

Definition: The number of times that company personnel hear the transfer process mentioned during new product development or launch.

Purpose: To make sure that the suppliers and customers recognize that the company is using a formalized transfer process that is focused on supplier-
customer involvement and that the final product
should meet the needs of the customer. This metric
will show the value of using the transfer process in
the marketplace.

Goal: Prioritize the process.

Metric: Did the right resources get assigned to the
projects based on their priority?

Definition: Percentage of resources placed on the right
priority project.

Purpose: Measure the effectiveness of prioritizing
projects.

Goal: Increase the economic value added for the company.

Metric: Actual versus forecast economic value.

Definition: Percentage increase in the return on equity versus the amount forecast.

Purpose: To determine the economic value of using a
formalized transfer process.

Tool 13: Process Audit

A process audit provides for continuous improvement of
the transfer process and the overall quality of projects. The

audit occurs a number of years after the new product has been launched. At that time, the transfer team is brought back to reexamine how the project proceeded and check the financials to see if the project is returning to the company the kind of money originally projected. The continuous improvement occurs when the projected returns, market acceptance, and project cycle time are compared. The difference, or variance, must be explained to provide future teams insight into their projects.

Case Study: New Drug Process Audit

XYZ Co. used a formal transfer process and cross-functional team for all its new drug compounds. A new drug, number 12567AP, was developed three years ago, and management has requested a process audit from Zach, the transfer team leader. Zach calls his team together, and together they begin to gather the data necessary to perform an audit. The team consults with the company controller, and she reports the financial numbers for drug 12567AP. Figure 3-11 shows all financial calculations from early in the project until just recently.

Figure 3-11. Financial audit for Project 12567AP.

Date Analyzed	Stage	Product Volume, in K	Price, in $	Revenues, in $K	Project NPV, in $M
January-00	0	1,000	$25.25	$25,250	$150
March-00	2	2,000	$25.00	$50,000	$300
June-00	4	2,000	$17.50	$35,000	$200
September-00	Launch	2,000	$20.00	$40,000	$225
September-04	4 years after	1,450	$21.50	$31,175	$180

The first financial estimate projected the volume of the new drug at 1 million. However, with a projected selling price of $25.25 each and considering the cost of manufacturing, the net present value (NPV) was a positive $150 million. (NPV as an economic measure of merit is described in detail in Chapter 4.) This was projected to be a very attractive project, and it proceeded on the merits of this early financial calculation.

As the project proceeded, the projected volumes doubled, with the selling price or projected value falling slightly. The effect on NPV was an increase, and the project proceeded through commercialization. Four years later, the actual number received from the company controller showed the volume to be slightly lower than finally projected but higher than the original projection. The perceived value in the marketplace was slightly higher than the final projected $20.00 but lower than the original projected $25.25. The net effect on actual NPV was $180 million versus the original $150 million. The financial audit was very positive. The new drug was indeed a success in the marketplace, and the company profited slightly more than originally projected. This brought a smile to Zach's face!

Zach then proceeded to summarize the team commitment for this project and its overall success. The learnings taken from this project by upper management were all positive. This is not always the case; nevertheless, continuous improvement comes from understanding mistakes as well as successes.

Questions beyond the financial outcome of the project are important for continuous improvement: How did the team perform? How did the Stage-Gate process work? How were the communications? and How well was the product received in the marketplace? Here are some questions that the audit team might explore in each area:

Team Performance

- When was the team put together?

- What functions were present?

- Were the team responsibilities defined and carried out?

- How did the individuals perform?

The Stage-Gate Process

- Did the stages have enough detail?

- Were critical dates identified?

- Was the project on schedule? If not, why not?

- What did the team do when the project got off schedule?

- Were the resources allocated well?

Product

- Did the product meet customer expectations?

- Were there any product changes necessary?

- Were there start-up problems?

This process audit can be enlightening and also provide important feedback to management to allow the company to improve continuously toward product transfer excellence.

NOTES

1. "Time—The Next Dimension of Quality," video featuring John Guaspari and Edward Hay, Rath and Strong Management Consultants, American Management Association, 1993.

2. Ibid.

3. Paula M. Noaker, "Manufacturing by Design," *Manufacturing Engineering* (June 1992).

4. Robert G. Cooper, *Winning at New Products: Accelerating the Process from Idea to Launch, 3d Edition* (Reading, Mass.: Perseus Books, 2001).

5. Ibid.

Chapter 4

Financial Tools

Financial estimates of the value and cost of the project are critical elements in the decision whether to launch the effort or to continue development. Financial estimates are used for the following reasons:

- To estimate the economic benefits to the business

- To compare the attractiveness of projects to assign priority and allocate resources

- To identify the areas with the greatest economic benefit

- To compare options within a project and select the most attractive one

ECONOMIC JUSTIFICATION

Three tools are useful to accomplishing these elements: Tool 14, Cost Estimating; Tool 15, Economic Measures of Merit; and Tool 16, Setting Project Priorities.

Tool 14: Cost Estimating

When developing a new product, it is difficult to estimate the cost to manufacture the final product. Nevertheless, it is vital to the success of the company that the value in the marketplace and the costs to manufacture are at least estimated. These numbers are then modified as more information about the product and its manufacture are known. Therefore, it is important to be able to estimate product costs with limited data and have a model for updating as the project advances. The economic analysis comparing risk versus reward throughout the project will ensure increased profitability for the company.

After reviewing thousands of costs sheets for a myriad of products, I have developed a cost-estimating model that can predict costs within 10 percent. In the process of this work, I determined that 90 to 95 percent of all total costs are represented by seven costs:

- Materials

- Labor

- Utilities

- Maintenance

- Plant overheads

- Depreciation, taxes, and insurance

- General and administrative

In searching for the drivers that were common for each of the seven costs, I identified three items with the greatest impact on costs: materials, total capital investment, and labor. The task then was to develop common factors that, when multiplied by these three common drivers, would result in an accurate and reliable estimate. If this could be done, estimating the product costs early in a project and updating them throughout the life of the project could be substantially simplified. The following pages will discuss the common cost drivers and factors used to obtain a good estimate.

Materials

Use a thorough list of all materials in the product that you are estimating to calculate the quantity used in the final shipped product and the material price in dollars per unit or per pound. This number must be multiplied by the process yield. The process yield is essentially scrap, or the number of bad parts that are made in order to make a quantity of good ones. Someone has to pay for this wasted material, and usually the cost is passed on to the customer.

The equation for estimating material is material price times quantity produced (units) divided by yield:

$$\text{Price} \times (\text{units}/\text{yield})$$

The following case studies show this formula in action.

Case Study: Total Materials Used

The vice president of engineering at Laser Co. has been given the task of identifying areas of improvement for a laser probe, one of many products produced by the company. He thinks that material costs are probably high for the probe, but nobody at Laser Co. really knows for sure.

Bill, an industrial engineer, was given the assignment to calculate material costs for the probe. The probe sells for $600, and everyone believes that materials probably make up a high percentage of production costs. Bill was asked to quantify the probe material costs, so the first thing he did was to put together a bill of materials:

Bill of Materials: Laser Probe

Fiber-optic cable	2 feet
Flex tube (plastic)	2 feet
Spring action mechanism	
Laser cutters	(2)

Bill knew the unit price for each of the materials. He asked the operations manager to provide him with all material yields. He also knew that 3,500 probes were assembled yearly (see Figure 4-1). He calculated the composite cost using the strategic costing equation for estimating materials:

$$P \times (U/Y).$$

Figure 4-1. Calculation of composite material costs.

Materials	Unit Price	Quantity Used	Yield	Total Annual Costs
Fiber-optic cable	$75	3,500	90%	$291,667
Flex tube	$5	3,500	95%	$18,421
Spring action mechanism	$22	3,500	100%	$77,000
Laser cutters (2)	$215	3,500	97%	$775,773
Total annual composite cost				$1,162,861

Dividing this cost of $1,162,861 by 3,500 salable probes results in material costs per probe of $332.25.

This study confirmed that the vice president was correct. The material costs of $332.25 were 20 percent higher than expected. This was therefore one area of improvement for Laser Co. The vice president set a target for improvement of the probe of $300 for materials.

Case Study: Total Materials Used

Susan, a chemist at Barnes Chemical, was asked to establish the costs of the materials to manufacture 1 million pounds of fiber B per year. First, she had to calculate the total quantity of materials used. She did this by taking the quantity of material per pound of fiber times the 1 million annual pounds produced. After talking with plant operations personnel about material yields, she put together the material cost sheet shown in Figure 4-2 on page 68.

Labor

Calculating an estimate of yearly labor costs requires knowing two things: the total number of people directly working on the product or service and their average wage rate.

The number of people directly working on the product or service may be estimated for the new product or obtained by counting them during a tour of the supplier's plant. You could also ask directly or make an educated estimate.

The average wage rate may be obtained by asking the local chamber of commerce for the average regional pay scale. Again, you could also just ask your supplier's facility tour guide.

Figure 4-2. Annual cost of manufacturing yarn B.

Equation:	P x	(U			/ Y)	= Cost
Materials	Unit Price	Quantity/ Pound Of Fiber	Fiber Sold	Quantity Used	Yield	Annual Costs
Solvent	$2/lb	.25	1 million	.25 million	.75	$666,666
Glycol	$2/lb	.75	1 million	.75 million	.80	$1,875,000
Additives	$5/lb	.10	1 million	.10 million	.95	$526,315
Stabilizers	$20/lb	.05	1 million	.05 million	.90	$900,000
				Total annual composite costs:		$3,967,981
				Material costs per pound of yarn B:		$3.97

Once you have an estimate of the number of people directly working on the product or service and their pay scale, determining the annual labor cost will require adjusting those figures for vacation time, relief hours during the workday, benefits, and supervision. Each of these is adjusted by a multiplying factor.

■ *Vacation factor = 1.11.* Vacation time must be included as an addition to the yearly labor cost calculation, because while the operator is on paid vacation, another person must be paid to perform the operation or service. The multiplying factor is 1.11, which is calculated assuming an average of three weeks paid vacation and 11 paid holidays, or 26 days, which is 208 hours. Assuming one shift of operation, there are 2,080 hours in a year (8 hours a day times 5 days per week times 52 weeks per year). The 1.11 multiplier is calculated by subtracting 208 hours from 2,080 and dividing that number into 2,080.

Hours per year − vacation/holiday = Total hours worked

$$2,080 - 208 = 1,872$$
$$2,080/1,872 = 1.11$$

■ *Relief factor = 1.23.* The relief factor builds in some cost to compensate for less than 8 hours production in an 8-hour day. Operators take lunch, rest room, and communication breaks throughout the day. Although they are paid for 8 hours, they actually work on the average of only 6.5 hours a day. This multiplying factor is 1.23 (8 divided by 6.5).

■ *Benefits factor = 1.3.* Employees are entitled to health care benefits. This is about 30 percent of their base pay and must be included in a yearly labor cost calculation. Therefore, the multiplier for benefits is 1.3.

■ *Supervision factor = 1.3.* A calculation for first-line supervision should be included in an annual labor cost calculation. This calculation assumes 1 first-line supervisor for every 10 operators. The supervisor is paid at a higher rate than the operators, so the multiplier to account for first-line supervision is 1.3.

An accurate estimate of annual labor costs is number of people, times the average wage rate, times total hours in a year worked (if the product or service were produced in less than a year, the number would be the actual hours worked), times the vacation, relief, benefit, and supervision factors. The equation looks like this:

Number of operators × $ wage rate × 2,080 × (1.11*1.23*1.3*1.3)

Approximately 4,800

Case Study: Estimating Labor to Produce Scanning Instruments

Mark has worked as a buyer for St. Michael's Hospital for 24 years. Mark has always taken pride in providing the hospital staff with the finest-quality products available. In a recent group meeting, Mark's superiors discussed how St. Michael's Hospital would be evolving into a profit-making organization at the beginning of the next year.

As a precursor to this change, Mark's supervisor requested that he analyze two suppliers of scanning instruments prior to St. Michael's purchasing 200 of these units to be used throughout the hospital. Comparable units have been selling for approximately $4,500.

Mark's strategy for getting the best price on the scanning instruments is to check with the finance department first to determine the maximum affordable price and then to visit each supplier to estimate their costs. Then, using strategic costing calculations to guide him, he will negotiate the best deal for the hospital.

His visit to the finance department was shocking. It turned out that in order to earn a slight profit at the end of three years (the predetermined life of the units), the maximum affordable price for the instruments should be no more than $5,000. But recent quotes from two suppliers for a quantity of 200 were $5,150 and $5,400 per unit.

Mark then set up a visit to each supplier's plant. He also asked two of his coworkers, one from engineering and one from accounting, to join him on the plant tours. Mark wanted to determine each supplier's labor costs because he believed that the assembly of the scanning instruments was probably very labor intensive and realized that his estimate of labor costs would be critical. He asked his coworkers to count the people they saw during their tour—both those assembling the instruments and those who appeared to be working directly on the units.

After the tours, Mark compared his operator count with those of his coworkers. Some workers appeared to be doing multiple operations, and still others were working on several completely different products during the day, so making the tallies was a little difficult. Nevertheless, you can see in Figure 4-3 that the differences among Mark and his coworkers were not that great at either plant. Each supplier worked on a two-shift basis, so the number they counted would be multiplied by two. Supplier B appeared to be considerably more automated.

Mark next calculated total labor costs for each supplier. He checked at the local chamber of commerce for average assembly worker wages in each supplier's area. The average wage rate for Supplier A is $17.50 per hour and for Supplier B is $21.00 per hour.

Figure 4-3. Labor count for scanning instrument suppliers.

Total Operators	Mark's Count	Engineering Count	Accounting Count	Average
Supplier A	52	56	48	52
Supplier B	34	32	32	32

Each supplier produces 1,000 instruments per shift per year, so each could produce the 200 instruments that St. Michael's would order using only 10 percent of the total yearly labor.

$$200/(1,000 \text{ instruments/shift/year} \times 2 \text{ shifts/day}) = .1 \ (10\%)$$

When Mark made his labor calculations for each supplier (see Figure 4-4), he found that he was right: The labor costs for the scanning machines were considerable. Of its $5,400 price tag, Supplier A's labor costs were $2,184 per unit ($436,800 divided by 200 instruments). Supplier B was indeed more automated so Mark was a little puzzled at this point as to why its price was $5,150 when its labor costs were only $1,613 per unit ($322,560 divided by 200 instruments).

Mark now felt confident to begin negotiations with each supplier to try and reduce the price per instrument and enable St. Michael's hospital to obtain a desired profit. Because of his efforts, he was able to secure a quote for the 200 instruments from Supplier B at a cost of $4,650.

Figure 4-4. Labor calculations for scanning instrument suppliers.

		Annual Labor Costs
Supplier A	52 x $17.50 x 4,800 x 10%	$436,800
Supplier B	32 x $21.00 x 4,800 x 10%	$322,560

Utilities

Utilities include all the power associated with running the equipment used to produce the product. All utilities are based on the equipment and therefore are driven by the investment in that equipment. By studying thousands of product cost sheets for a myriad of products and using total investment as the driver, I determined the investment percentage of annual utilities costs: 2 percent. Out of the 1,500 projects studied, 500 had annual utility costs of 2 percent. Although the percentage had a fairly wide standard deviation, 2 percent was indeed the mean, as seen in Figure 4-5.

The number that represents total investment is the total replacement investment for the equipment being used plus the investment needed to install the equipment. You must estimate not only what it would cost to buy the equipment new, but multiply it by three to include installation, project management, and facilities associated with getting the equipment ready to run.

In estimating a supplier's equipment investment, it's always good practice to take someone from engineering along on a visit to suppliers. That person will recognize which equipment is being used to produce the product and can either estimate the equipment's new value or request a quote from the vendor of the equipment. (The vendor's name is always prominently placed on any major piece of equipment.) For example, when estimating the

Figure 4-5. Utility costs.

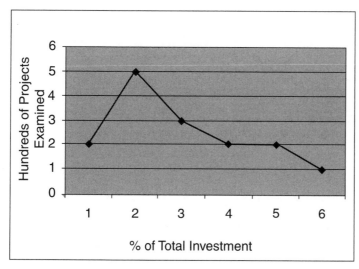

annual utilities costs for a 1,000-ton injection molding press made by Cincinnati Milacron, I first requested a vendor quote. The quote was $250,000, which is the replacement investment. I then multiplied replacement investment by three to account for installation and facilities (power, lighting, and heating and air-conditioning), for a total investment of $750,000. This is the number that drives the estimate for utilities. The investment driver is also used to estimate maintenance and depreciation, so taking the time to develop a good-quality investment number is essential and well worth the effort.

To calculate the annual utilities cost, take 2 percent of the total investment. In the example of the 1,000-ton press, the annual utilities cost would be calculated as follows:

$$
\begin{aligned}
\text{Utilities} &= \text{Total investment (TI)} \times .02 \\
&= \$750,000 \times .02 \\
&= \$15,000 \text{ per year}
\end{aligned}
$$

If the injection molding press was used only a portion of the year, then the annual cost of utilities would be multiplied by the portion of the year the equipment was actually being used. In the example, if the injection molding press was being used to manufacture parts that your company purchased and those parts could be made in one-tenth of the year, the utilities would be one-tenth the annual cost, or $1,500 for the utilities cost estimate to make your parts.

Maintenance

Maintenance includes both labor and materials to keep the process that is making the product or service, such as a mainframe computer, maintained and producing in an efficient manner. This element of cost is directly related to the investment in the equipment used. The estimate of annual maintenance cost is calculated at 6 percent of the total investment.

$$\text{Maintenance} = .06 \times \text{total investment}$$

Plant Overheads

Overheads include all the indirect costs associated with the production of the product or service. Although the elements in overhead vary by company and industrial sector, overhead typically includes the following elements:

- General plant burden

- Overtime

- Plant administration (management and staff)

- Employee relations

- Medical

- Fire and plant protection

- Internal transportation (shipping and receiving)

- Carrying and acquisition costs

- Communications

- Computers and telephone systems

- Engineering assistance to operations

- Grounds upkeep

- Cafeteria

The problem with assigning or allocating overhead costs to a product or service when there is more than one product or service produced at a given location is defining the costs to be distributed correctly. A good formula for estimating for overheads is .75 times labor:

$$\text{Overhead} = .75 \times \text{labor}$$

Depreciation, Taxes, and Insurance

Depreciation is one of the most misunderstood concepts associated with cost sheet and cash flow analysis. *Depreciation* is an accounting element, a noncash cost in total costs. Basically it is an investment incentive that the government gives to corporations to encourage them to continue to invest. Fixed assets that are invested in have a useful life, which is usually 10 years. When figuring out investment depreciation, if you know the replacement investment of the facility (equipment and building), it will be 10 percent of that value per year assuming 10 years of useful life. Therefore, the equation to estimate the investment depreciation is:

$$\text{Investment depreciation} = 10\% \times \text{total capital investment}$$

To this calculation add property taxes and insurance on the facility at 1 percent and the final equation will be:

$$\text{Depreciation, taxes, and insurance} = 11\% \times \text{total investment}$$

General and Administrative Costs

Following are some typical general and administrative costs:

- Selling expenses (personal selling expenses such as travel, salaries, commissions, sales office rental, service, advertising, promotions, and other marketing functions)

- Executive compensation

- Staff departments

- Legal

- Finance

- Purchasing

- Accounting

- Central engineering

- Office space

- Insurance

- Property taxes

- Clerical

The allocation of these expenses is even harder to do than the allocation of overheads and is probably not worth the effort. As a rule of thumb, you can obtain the annual reports of your company, your supplier, and your competitor and calculate the percentage of general and administrative versus all other expenses. This will usually be approximately 15% of the total of all other costs.

General and administrative expenses =
15% × total expenses

Figure 4-6 is the Steadman Company's income statement. In this example, the total expenses (cash expenses and depreciation) were $3,000 and the general and administrative (G&A) expenses were $500, or 16 percent of total expenses. If you have access to this kind of information (which can be found in the annual report), calculate the actual G&A as a percentage of total expenses and use that calculation when you are estimating total costs. If this information is not available, a good estimate for G&A expenses is 15 percent of total expenses.

Figure 4-6. Steadman Company income statement.

	Amount	Revenues
		4,500
-Cash Expenses	$2,500	
-G&A Expenses	500	
-Depreciation	500	
Earnings Before Taxes		1,000
-Taxes	400	
Net Income		600

Case Study: Widget International

You have requested a quote from Widget International for 500,000 widgets. You know that to be competitive, you must pay under $4 each. Each widget weighs one pound, and you estimate their cost using this information (assume a 10 percent markup):

Material Price	$1/lb
Process Yield	90%
Operators Needed	4 (1 shift) @$15/hour
Total Investment	$2,000,000

Widget International has quoted $4.13. Figure 4-7 is provided for you to do your own calculations before looking at our quote for this case study. Compare your cost estimate with the quote seen in Figure 4-8.

Summary of Equations

Figure 4-9 summarizes the cost-estimating equations.

Tool 15: Economic Measures of Merit

There are three economic measures of merit: net present value (NPV), discounted payback period (DPP), and internal rate of return (IRR). NPV and DPP will be discussed here; IRR, which is used to prioritize projects, will be discussed under Tool 16 (setting project priorities). These measures of merit help define the associated return and risk on projects.

NPV is a representation in today's dollars of what a company will earn on its investment after 10 years of operation, plus earning the cost of capital on the investment for the 10 years. If the NPV is positive, additional

Figure 4-7. Cost-estimating worksheet.

TOTAL MATERIALS USED		
P x (U/Y) [Price per unit times (units divided by yield)]		
UTILITIES		
TI x .02 [Total investment times 2%]		
LABOR		
# x $ x 4,800 [Number of operators times hourly rate times 4,800]		
MAINTENANCE		
TI x .06 [Total investment times 6%]		
OVERHEADS		
L x .75 [Labor times 75%]		
DEPRECIATION, TAXES, AND INSURANCE		
TI x .11 [Total investment times 11%]		
Subtotal 1		
GENERAL AND ADMINISTRATIVE		
Subtotal 1 x .15 [Subtotal 1 times 15%]		
Total Costs		

money will go into the company coffers. If the NPV is negative, the company will not be earning enough to defray the cost of capital on the investment, and it should not be made. Using cash flow analysis will tell a company whether to proceed with the transfer project.

Discounted payback period shows management how long the company's money will be at risk before earning a profit.

Figure 4-8. Widget International spreadsheet.

Widget International		
		Widget Cost Estimate
Total Materials	P times (U/Y)	$555,555
Power	TI times .02	$40,000
Labor	# times $ times 4,800	$288,000
Maintenance	TI times .06	$120,000
Overheads	L times .75	$216,000
Depreciation, Taxes, and Insurance	TI times .11	$220,000
Subtotal		$1,439,555
General and Administrative	Subtotal times .15	$215,933

Total Costs:	$1,655,488
Unit Cost per Widget:	$3.31

Figure 4-10 shows a typical 10-year cash flow curve. The NPV in year 10 is $600K—a positive number, which is good. The project investment, plus a certain percentage each year (the cost of capital), is also paid off in a little over four years, which is the discounted payback period. The last piece of information on this curve is the amount of risk, which is the minimum number, or −$600K. If a

Figure 4-9. Summary of cost-estimating equations.

CATEGORY	EQUATION	LEGEND
Total materials	$P \times (U/Y)$	P = Price U = Unit Y = Yield
Utilities	$TI \times 0.02$	TI = Total investment
Labor	# x $ x 4,800	# = Number of operators $ = Hourly rate
Maintenance	$TI \times 0.06$	TI = Total investment
Plant overheads	$L \times 0.75$	L = Labor
Depreciation	$TI \times 0.11$	TI = Total investment
General and administrative	15% x Total expense	

transfer team calculated this potential cash flow curve for a project, they would be working on an excellent project.

Performing a Cash Flow Analysis

Now let's turn to the process for calculating and performing a cash flow analysis. To construct a discounted cumulative cash flow takes three steps:

Step 1: Estimate the cash flow streams produced by the project for 10 years.

Step 2: Discount the streams by the cost of capital, so that all streams are in today's dollars.

Step 3: Cumulate the discounted cash flow streams and plot.

Step 1: Estimate the Cash Flow Streams. Cash flow streams may be estimated each year by using the methodology below:

Revenue

  Minus cash expenses

  Minus depreciation

Equals Before Tax Operating Income

  Minus taxes

Equals Net Income

  Plus depreciation

  Minus capital investment

Equals Year-End Cash Flow

Figure 4-10. Ten-year cash flow analysis.

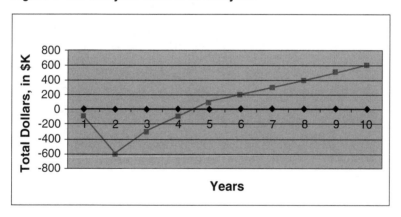

Obtain a sales forecast from the operating department in which the product is being developed, or have your team develop a best guess for projected sales (a great place to use the group consensus tool!). For cash expenses, use either a worksheet on cash expenses from your accounting department or the cost-estimating model from this book. Subtract cash expenses from revenue. Then subtract depreciation. Depreciation is a noncash cost; in other words, no cash changes hands. It is just a tax break the government affords companies to encourage reinvestment and economic growth. Using 10-year straight-line depreciation, the depreciation becomes $\frac{1}{10}$ of the total project capital investment.

The project investment must include all project-related work: engineering drawings and planning, buildings, installation of equipment, and project contingencies. If you know the price of the bare equipment for the project, the total project investment will usually be about two to three times that. Taxes include both state and federal income taxes on the operating income. Taxes usually run 35 to 40 percent for most companies. Subtract taxes from the operating income to yield net income, or the bottom line. Now, add depreciation back in. Remember that no money changes hands for depreciation. You just subtracted it from revenues so that no taxes are calculated on that amount. Then you have to add it back in to account for all monies earned. Subtract the total capital project investment in the first year only, and you have the yearly cash flow.

To make sure you understand the methodology for calculating cash flow, do the following problem in the space provided above Figure 4-11.

Calculate the first-year cash flow for the installation and operation of 100 ATM machines in Topeka, Kansas.

Expected revenues from the service charges and customer convenience are $3 million per year. It will take $1 million per year to maintain and operate the machines. Each machine requires a total investment of $50,000. Assume taxes at a 50 percent rate and depreciation at 10 percent of total investment. The answer is in Figure 4-11.

Figure 4-11. ATM cash flow answer.

Year 1, in $ millions	
Revenues	$3.0
Minus, Cash Expenses	1.0
Minus, Depreciation	.5
Before-Tax Operating Income	1.5
Minus, Income Taxes @ 50%	.75
Net Income	.75
Plus, Depreciation	.5
Minus, Investments	5.0
Year-End Cash Flow	(3.75)

Step 2: Discount the Streams by the Cost of Capital and **Step 3: Cumulate the Discounted Cash Flow Streams and Plot.** The time value of money is an important concept in economics. It reflects the fact that a dollar today is worth more than a dollar one year from now, because that dollar may be invested to earn a profit. By discounting each year's cash flow stream to yield the value in today's dollars, we can compare everything on an apples-to-apples basis. This way, we avoid giving too much credence to a project with large cash flow streams projected far into the future.

Calculating today's value of a future amount of money is called discounting and always results in a smaller sum of money today.

Current value = future value divided by (1 + interest rate)

As an example, the value of $1,100 discounted at 10% for one year is:

Current value = $1,100 divided by (1 + 10%)= $1,000

For periods longer than one year, the value (1 + interest rate) is taken to the exponent of the number of years.

These discount values can be found in the table of present value in Figure 4-12.

Using the present value table, take the year-end cash stream and look down the left-hand column until you get to the year of the stream. Then go to the column under the discounted rate used. Use as an example $1,000

Figure 4-12. Present value table.

Periods, n	4%	6%	8%	10%	12%	15%	20%	30%	50%
1	0.962	0.943	0.926	0.909	0.893	0.870	0.833	0.769	0.667
2	0.925	0.890	0.857	0.826	0.797	0.756	0.694	0.592	0.444
3	0.889	0.840	0.794	0.751	0.712	0.658	0.579	0.455	0.296
4	0.855	0.792	0.735	0.683	0.636	0.572	0.482	0.350	0.198
5	0.822	0.747	0.681	0.621	0.567	0.497	0.402	0.269	0.132
6	0.790	0.705	0.630	0.564	0.507	0.432	0.335	0.207	0.088
7	0.760	0.665	0.583	0.513	0.452	0.376	0.279	0.159	0.059
8	0.731	0.627	0.540	0.467	0.404	0.327	0.233	0.123	0.039
9	0.703	0.592	0.500	0.424	0.361	0.284	0.194	0.094	0.026
10	0.676	0.558	0.463	0.386	0.322	0.247	0.162	0.073	0.017
11	0.650	0.527	0.429	0.350	0.287	0.215	0.135	0.056	0.012
12	0.625	0.497	0.397	0.319	0.257	0.187	0.112	0.043	0.008
13	0.601	0.469	0.368	0.290	0.229	0.163	0.093	0.033	0.005
14	0.577	0.442	0.340	0.263	0.205	0.141	0.078	0.025	0.003
15	0.555	0.417	0.315	0.239	0.183	0.123	0.065	0.020	0.002
16	0.534	0.394	0.292	0.218	0.163	0.107	0.054	0.015	0.002
17	0.513	0.371	0.270	0.198	0.146	0.093	0.045	0.012	0.001
18	0.494	0.350	0.250	0.180	0.130	0.081	0.038	0.009	0.001
19	0.475	0.331	0.232	0.164	0.116	0.070	0.031	0.007	
20	0.456	0.312	0.215	0.149	0.104	0.061	0.026	0.005	
25	0.375	0.233	0.146	0.092	0.059	0.030	0.010	0.001	
30	0.308	0.174	0.099	0.057	0.033	0.015	0.004		
40	0.208	0.097	0.046	0.022	0.011	0.004	0.001		
50	0.141	0.054	0.021	0.009	0.003	0.001			

earned 4 years from now with a discount rate of 12%. Go
down to 4 (the "periods" column) and over to the "12%"
column. The discount factor is 0.636. Now multiply $1,000
times 0.636, to get $636. A cash flow stream of $1,000 four
years from now with a discount rate of 12% would be
worth only $636 today.

How do you know what discount rate to use? I've
referred to the cost of capital before. The cost of capital is
the weighted average cost of financing from all sources
(debt and equity):

$$\text{Equity } 15\% \times \tfrac{2}{3} = 10\%$$
$$\text{Debt } 7\% \times \tfrac{1}{3} = 2\%$$
$$\text{Weighted average cost of capital} = 12\%$$

Most companies use 12 percent as their cost of capital.
Discounting at the cost of capital measures the return from
an investment against the cost to fund it. A positive NPV
means the project's discounted cash flow exceeds the cost
of capital.

Suppose you won $1 million in the lottery. The lottery
commission tells you that you will receive $200,000 at the
end of this year and $200,000 for the next four years, or
you may take a lump sum right now of $800,000. Which
would you choose? Assume if you were receiving the
$800,000 now that you could invest it and receive 10 per-
cent per year for the five years. Use the worksheet in Figure 4-13 to work out your solution.

Figure 4-13. Lottery worksheet.

End of Year	1	2	3	4	5	Total
Payments	$200,000	$200,000	$200,000	$200,000	$200,000	$1,000,000
Discount Factor @ 10%						
Annual NPV						

The answer is in Figure 4-14. If you received $200,000 at the end of the first year and every year thereafter for five years, you would receive $758,000 in today's dollars. You would be better off taking the $800,000 lump sum today.

Figure 4-14. Lottery problem solution.

End of Year	1	2	3	4	5	Total
Payments	$200,000	$200,000	$200,000	$200,000	$200,000	$1,000,000
Discount Factor @ 10%	0.909	0.826	0.751	0.683	0.621	
Annual NPV	$181,800	$165,200	$150,200	$136,600	$124,200	$758,000

Now let's work through a cash flow problem. Assume we have already used the cash flow methodology from Step 1 and calculated five years of cash flow streams at −$1,000, $250, $500, $1,000, and $1,500. Calculate the present value at 12 percent cost of capital by discounting the streams by 12 percent so that all the streams are in today's dollars. Step 2: Cumulate the discounted streams to yield the present value in year 5 (Step 3) using Figure 4-15. The answer is in Figure 4-16.

The NPV of this project would be $1,149, with a break-even between years 3 and 4. This would be a good project.

Tool 16: Setting Project Priorities

To prioritize projects and maximize profitability, use IRR. The IRR provides the actual percentage earned on the investment per year. There is no way to calculate this amount directly. You must calculate the NPV; if it is positive, try a higher interest rate, and recalculate the NPV. Keep doing that until the NPV is zero. At that point you have the IRR. It is an interactive calculation.

Figure 4-15. Cash flow worksheet.

End of Year	Cash Flow	Discount Factor	Discounted Cash Flow	Cumulative
1	($1,000)			
2	$250			
3	$500			
4	$1,000			
5	$1,500			

Figure 4-16. Cash flow solution.

End of Year	Cash Flow	Discount Factor	Discounted Cash Flow	Cumulative
1	($1,000)	0.893	($893)	($893)
2	$250	0.797	$199	($694)
3	$500	0.712	$356	($338)
4	$1,000	0.636	$636	($298)
5	$1,500	0.567	$851	$1,149

Using the example in Figure 4-17, the IRR would be calculated somewhere between 12 percent because it had a positive NPV and 50 percent. At 50 percent, the NPV is just negative. Extrapolating to get the actual IRR value, the result is approximately 45 percent.

IRR is an important value. When companies have limited resources, the projects must be prioritized. IRR is a great tool to do just that.

In order to maximize profitability, a company should prioritize projects based on IRR. It should choose to do the highest-IRR project first, the second-highest IRR second, and so forth. This will give a project portfolio with great returns.

Figure 4-17. Calculating internal rate of return.

Calculated @ 12%

End of Year	Cash Flow	Discount Factor	Discounted Cash Flow	Cumulative
1	($1,000)	0.893	($893)	($893)
2	$250	0.797	$199	($694)
3	$500	0.712	$356	($338)
4	$1,000	0.636	$636	($298)
5	$1,500	0.567	$851	$1,149

Calculated @ 50%

End of Year	Cash Flow	Discount Factor	Discounted Cash Flow	Cumulative
1	($1,000)	0.667	($667)	($893)
2	$250	0.444	$111	($556)
3	$500	0.296	$148	($408)
4	$1,000	0.198	$198	($210)
5	$1,500	0.132	$198	($12)

Case Study: Company XYZ

Company XYZ has $800,000 in its capital forecast for next year and must prioritize from the projects shown in Figure 4-18.

Figure 4-18. Potential transfer projects.

Project	Total Investment	NPV ($K)	IRR %
Cleaning robot	100	50	20
Lightning detector	300	−30	5
Project A	75	70	30
Arrester	225	85	20
Terminator	225	45	15
Project B	350	200	25
Steam assist	25	90	60

By choosing the steam assist project with a 60 percent IRR first, Project A with a 30 percent IRR second, Project B with a 25 percent IRR third, and either the cleaning robot project or the arrester project both with 20 percent IRR's fourth, the overall return for Company XYZ is maximized.

After these projects, Company XYZ would be above its capital forecast and would choose not to do project lightning detector and project terminator. Project terminator appears to be only marginally profitable and project lightning detector would actually earn lower than the cost of capital for Company XYZ. The rack-up of these projects may be seen in Figure 4-19.

Figure 4-19. Prioritized transfer projects.

	IRR%	TI
Steam assist	60	25
Project A	30	75
Project B	25	350
Arrester	20	225
Cleaning robot	20	100

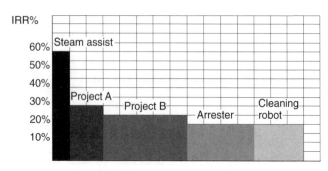

Chapter 5

Developing and Implementing a Formal Transfer Process

The 16 tools will help teams successfully transfer a product or idea from R&D through manufacturing and product launch. These tools have been used to address the common keys to team success: clear objectives, cross-functional team approach, robust design and product, structured methodology, and economic attractiveness. The 16 tools alone will help any team accomplish its goal. However, for a company to benefit truly from these tools, a transfer process must be developed, documented, communicated, and implemented throughout the organization.

The most important component of the process is the champion. Without a person who has the passion to see a successful transfer process come to fruition, the process will not happen. All my success in consulting has come when an individual has approached me to help develop a process. These individuals were the company's champion. Since you are reading this book, I assume you have such a passion for your company's success in this kind of endeavor. The development of a successful transfer process at your company may start with you.

Any improvement means change. A transfer process, no matter how good for the organization, will initially be plagued with skepticism. Moreover,

Any change is a perceived threat to security.

There will always be someone who will look at the suggested change as a threat to their security.

Now the door is wide open for the unpleasant conclusion. What is the unavoidable result when you threaten somebody's security?

Emotional resistance!

. . . We can only overcome emotion with a stronger emotion.[1]

Enter the champion. A champion has the drive necessary to counter the feeling of resistance the organization will have. A champion radiates positive emotion and views the project as his or her "baby." When improvement is involved, the powerful emotion of the champion can overcome the resistance of many.

When the champion gains acceptance for the new process, it is best to involve a cross-functional team in the development of its structure. It is vital to have the structure documented so the same process is followed every time. As the process evolves into an accepted and valuable model, it is used as a guide for all new products.

Once the team is put in place, it can formulate the process using seven steps.

DEVELOPING A PROCESS

Seven steps lead to the development of a skeleton of the final process. The figures referred to in the text are gathered at the end of this chapter.

Step 1: List the top four to six functions within your company. This list will help identify which functions should be included in the cross-functional transfer team. Two functions that appear on all company's lists are R&D and manufacturing. Go to Figure 5-1 now and fill it out for your company.

Step 2: List the major stages within a generic project. Figure 5-2 lists sample project stages for various industries. These stages will be used to structure your Stage-Gate model. Figure 5-3 gives seven sample stages in a generic new product project: idea concept, bench tests, pilot plant tests, plant tests, construction, implementation, and the audit. Go to Figure 5-4 now and fill out the major stages in a generic project for your company.

Step 3: Put together a phase diagram with functional responsibility. This step combines the information collected for Steps 1 and 2 and plots the involvement of each function in each of the various stages. The chart will help an organization see which functions are needed when, and from which function a probable project leader will emerge. Figure 5-5 shows a sample. Go to Figure 5-6 now and fill it out for your company.

Step 4: Put together a deliverables list with responsibility and stages designated. By developing a list of deliverables necessary for the product to be fit for sale, you will make sure that every item is being considered as the project proceeds. One additional part of the worksheet that is not included in Tool 6 is the identification of the person or function responsible for execution of each deliverable and in which stage the task must be completed. This information will provide the data necessary to put together a Stage-Gate responsibility chart, which is the next step. Figure 5-7 shows a sample. Go to Figure 5-8 now and fill it out for your company.

Step 5: Use the information from the deliverables list to put together a Stage-Gate responsibility chart. This step is the completion of a Stage-Gate responsibility chart. This information is generic for all projects. Some projects might not need all the items completed, but most will. This chart will become the guidepost for all transfer teams. Since every team will be using this chart as a guide, it is imperative that it be a complete document. Figure 5-9 shows a sample. Go to Figure 5-10 now and fill it out for your company.

Step 6: Put together a skeleton of the process. Your company's development team may now think about the structure of the transfer process. The skeleton of this process should be documented so the structure may be presented to all employees. In developing the skeleton of the process, the brainstorming technique works exceptionally well. This technique allows the whole team to present their ideas. The diagram shown in Figure 5-11 is an actual process structure; it shows that the core team included people from the functions of manufacturing, R&D, sales, and quality assurance. Sketch out your company's process structure on Figure 5-12. The core team is depicted at the heart of the process, with the process manager shown as a resource to the core team as they go through the transfer process. This core team is led by the champion and has inputs from suppliers and customers. As the team uses the tools of a Stage-Gate methodology, it needs approval from the approval committee to proceed from one stage to the next. Notice that the structure puts the champion and the core team above management. The total responsibility for results lies with the core team. Management is involved only as a check and balance system.

Step 7: List the process objectives and process metrics. As the newly developed transfer process is implemented, it will be necessary to make minor changes. In order to measure if the transfer process is beneficial for your company, list the process objectives and the metrics to measure their success. A sample of process objectives and metrics may be seen in Figure 5-13. Fill out Figure 5-14 now.

The development of the transfer process is now complete and documented. It is recommended that the development team put the process flow documentation into a training notebook for all new product transfer teams to follow. The new product transfer manager becomes the "go to person" for any team as they transfer a new product. The Appendix contains a sample transfer notebook.

With the worksheets filled out for your company's needs, a formal development process may be developed that will lead to the following benefits:

"Reported up to 50 percent decrease in cycle time"

"Claimed major improvements in economic value added"

"Competitiveness increased"

"Team/individuals have a feeling of accomplishment"

"Audit feedback allows continuous improvement"

IMPLEMENTING A PROCESS

Implementation is a make-it-or-break-it occurrence. A development team may put together a totally logical and effective transfer process, but it will fail unless everyone within the organization—management and employees—buys in to it. The development team can make the implementation relatively painless by properly training everyone, gaining senior management support early on, and paying attention to the fact that a change in the corporate culture might be necessary.

Training

In many companies, people often overlook the need for training and developing people at the working level of a corporation. In some companies, the relationship between management and labor must be healed. It is poor strategy to assume that workers will automatically accept changes. Workers are normally willing to explore and implement change if they are trained in the new techniques.

Gaining Senior Management Support

Probably the greatest cause of a poor R&D transfer is a lack of senior management support.

Management should be involved by the champion in Stage 0 in order to get initial support to proceed. The Stage-Gate process then requires that management be updated before proceeding to the next stage.

In a transfer project where time to market is short, the gate reviews alone might be sufficient involvement of senior management. When transfer projects run for additional months, additional reviews and briefings may be necessary. It is important for the team to be aware of management support and do whatever is necessary to maintain it.

Changing the Company Culture

To change the company culture, the following are items to consider:

- Review the concept with upper management.

- Let the organization know that a development team is working on a transfer process (through bulletin boards or a newsletter, for example).

- Train the entire organization.

- Produce a process notebook.

- Announce a process manager.

- Publish a process newsletter.

- Publish metrics.

- Use banners, screen savers, photos, or anything else to announce the changed company culture.

NOTE

1. Eliyahu Goldratt, *Theory of Constraints* (North River Press, 1996), p. 10.

Figure 5-1. Worksheet for identifying top company functions.

Step1: List the top four to six functions within your company.

If you were putting together a diverse team within your company, list the functions that would be represented:

_____

_____

_____

_____

_____

_____

_____

Figure 5-2. Project stages for various industries.

Industry:	Electronic	Pharmaceutical	Chemical	Part Manufacture
Stages				
1	Business study and concept development	Business study and concept development	Business study and concept development	Business study and concept development
2	Feasibility demo	Laboratory development	Laboratory development	Bench top demo
3	Hard model	Toxicology studies	Formula development	Prototype
4	Pilot facility	Laboratory scale-up	Lab scale testing	Customer testing
5	Commercial production	FDA documentation	Beta testing	Commercial production
6	Audit	Pilot scale-up	Process development	Manufacturing audit
7		Clinical testing	Market development facility	
8		Commercial development	Commercial production	
9		Licensing	Manufacturing audit	
10		FDA approval		
11		Commercial production		
12		Audit		

Figure 5-3. Project stages example.

Step 2: List the major stages within a generic project.

Stages	Description
1	Idea Concept
2	Bench Tests
3	Pilot Plant Tests
4	Plant Tests
5	Construction
6	Implementation
7	Audit
8	
9	
10	

Figure 5-4. Project stages worksheet.

Step 2: List the major stages within a generic project.

Stages	Description
1	
2	
3	
4	
5	
6	
7	
8	
9	
10	

Figure 5-5. Functional involvement example.

Step 3: Put together a phase diagram with functional responsibility.

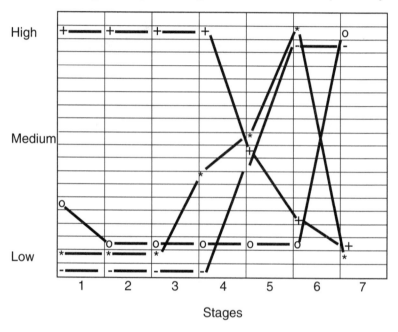

Stages

Symbol	Function
*	Engineering
o	Marketing
+	R&D
-	Manufacturing

Figure 5-6. Functional involvement worksheet.

Step 3: Put together a phase diagram with functional responsibility.

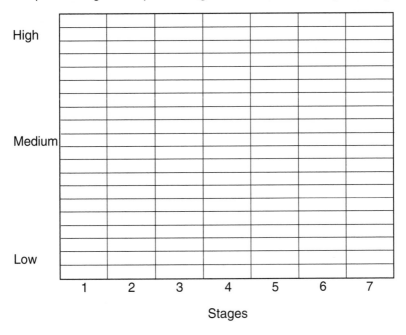

Stages

Symbol	Function
*	
o	
+	
-	

Figure 5-7. Deliverables list example.

Step 4: Put together a deliverables list with responsibility and
stages designated.

Item	Finished in What Stage	Responsibility
Internal Alpha Testing	3	R&D
External Beta Testing	5	Marketing
Product Safety	5	Manufacturing
Sales and Distribution Channels in Place	5	Marketing
Product Meets Regulatory Requirements	3	QA
Patent Inquiry	2	R&D
Patent Search	4	R&D
-		
-		
-		
-		
-		
-		
-		

Figure 5-8. Deliverables list worksheet.

Step 4: Put together a deliverables list with responsibility and
stages designated.

Item	Finished in What Stage	Responsibility

Figure 5-9. Stage-Gate responsibility chart example.

Step 5: Use the information from the deliverables list to put together a Stage-Gate responsibility chart.

CORE TEAM RESPONSIBILITIES OVERVIEW							
Stage 0	**Stage 1**	**Stage 2**	**Stage 3**	**Stage 4**	**Stage 5**	**Stage 6**	**Stage 7**
Pre-PRIDE	Idea Concept	Bench Tests	Pilot Plant Tests	Plant Tests	Construction	Implemen-tation	Post-PRIDE
Champion							
Idea Discussion	Begin Business Plan	Review Business Plan	Review Business Plan	Finalize Business Plan			Lead Audit
BOE Economics							PRIDE Metrics
Choose Core Team							
R & D							
Technical Feasibility	Preferred Alternative	Optimize Product & Process	Basic Data	Operational Basic Data		Facility Support	Audit R&D
Feasible Alternatives	Lab Samples	Lab Samples	Pilot Plant Samples (for Alpha Testing)	Plant Samples (for Beta Testing)		Debug	
Lab Samples	Supplier Contact			Finalize Formulas			
Initial Product Specifications	Patent Inquiry	Patent Search		Market Dev. Quantities			
Evironmental Implications			Environmental				
Sales							
Potential Market	Customer Evaluations	Customer Evaluations	Customer Evaluations	Customer Evaluations		Customer Satisfaction	Audit Sales
	Customer Contacts		Internal Alpha Testing	External Beta Testing		Market Launch	
				Begin Market Launch			
QA							
Sample Analysis	Sample Analysis	Sample Analysis	QA/Regulatory Requirements	Final Formulas		Sample Analysis	Audit QA
			Sample Analysis				
Manufacturing							
		Feasible Facility Alternatives	Facility Concept	Final Facilities Proj. Scope	Production Design	Mechanically Complete	Audit Manuf.
	High Spot Manuf. Costs		Begin SOP's	Final Manuf. Costs	Construct Facility	Start-Up Operations	
	High Spot Investment		Implement HACCP (edible only)	Final Capital Inv.	Finalize SOP's	Debug	

Figure 5-10. Stage-Gate responsibility chart worksheet.

Step 5: Use the information from the deliverables list to put together a Stage-Gate responsibility chart.

		TEAM RESPONSIBILITIES WORKSHEET					
Stage	Stage	Stage	Stage	Stage	Stage	Stage	Stage

Figure 5-11. Skeleton of the process example.

Step 6: Put together a skeleton of the process.

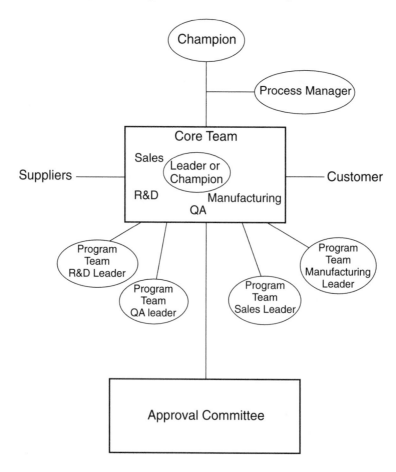

Figure 5-12. Skeleton of the process worksheet.

Step 6: Put together a skeleton of the process.

Figure 5-13. Process objectives and metrics example.

Step 7: List the process objectives and process metrics.

Transfer Process Objective	Metrics
Products to market faster	Actual vs. forecast cycle time
Lower development costs	Actual vs. forecast development costs
Upper management support	% of R&D budget allocated to transfer
Project prioritization	Number of people reassigned at gate reviews
	% core team turnover
Robust new offerings	Number of changes or rework of projects
More new product offerings	Number of transfer projects started

Figure 5-14. Process objectives and metrics worksheet.

Step 7: List the process objectives and process metrics.

Transfer Process Objective	Metrics

Chapter 6

Proliant, Inc.:
A Success Story

This chapter documents the chronology of events as a formal new product transfer process was developed and implemented by Proliant, Inc., which manufactures and markets protein products for the food, nutrition, human health, diagnostic, life science research, biopharmaceutical, and veterinary vaccine industries. The process occurred in winter 1997 and spring 1998, when Proliant's name was AMPC, Inc. (the name was changed in January 2001). Nevertheless, I use the new name throughout this chapter.

Proliant has three divisions, each focusing on specific market segments:

Proliant Ingredients, serving the food industry, including the dairy, bakery, nutrition, snack, meat/savory, and prepared-food markets

Proliant Health, serving the health and nutrition industry, including the dietary supplement, clinical nutrition, consumer health, and functional food markets

Proliant Biologicals, serving the diagnostic, life science research, biopharmaceutical, and veterinary vaccine markets

American Protein Company (APC), Proliant's sister company, is a leader in young animal nutrition, serving the calf nutrition, swine nutrition, pet nutrition, and aquaculture markets.

Proliant and APC are located in Ames, Iowa. A small company that is growing rapidly, its sales revenues in 1997 were about $100 million. In 1997, projected revenues for 2000 were about $250 million, or a compound annual growth rate of approximately 50 percent per year.

Proliant's commitment to R&D and new product excellence is evident. Its home page states, "Proliant is a world leader in protein fractionation because of a substantial investment in research and development. It is this commitment to continuous quality improvement that enables us to supply our customers with products that are 'Better Than the Best'" (*www.proliantinc.com*).

Here is its story.

May 15, 1996

Steve Welch, who at that time was moving from the director of finance to director of R&D, attended one of my seminars on successful new product transfer. Because he was just starting a new assignment in a new field, he did not fully grasp the importance of the seminar content he had just learned.

Fall 1997

About a year later, Steve recognized that given the way Proliant was growing and the additional responsibilities he was being asked to assume, he would benefit from a structured process to handle the new product concepts that were being developed. The company was growing so fast that the transfer of new product concepts to commercialization was becoming confusing and ineffective. A prime example of what was happening frequently is that when manufacturing finally stumbled through the testing and process commercialization, the marketing department was not ready for a new product launch. Steve called me and requested that I come out to Proliant to consult with the company's technical staff.

October 7, 1997

My proposal to Steve was to train and consult with a project team to develop a process before training all Proliant employees. Steve replied that the new product development process needed to be tailored to Proliant, which is what the team should do, but he also requested that I provide the documentation manual since nobody at Proliant had the time to document the process. Additionally, he requested that we pick an actual Proliant project that was near completion and would serve as a case study of an actual project taken through the new process. I agreed with Steve, and we set up our first meeting for January 9, 1998. After the first meeting, when objectives, plans, and timing were firmed up, I would submit a full estimate of the time necessary to complete the project.

January 9, 1998

I flew to Des Moines and met with Steve and the director

of human resources. Over dinner, I discussed a skeleton model of a transfer process (see Figure 6-1), and we agreed that the next day we would work with a prepicked team, which Steve had put together, to flesh out the model and the proposal and to agree on the scope of the project before proceeding.

We began the day with a tour of the Proliant research facility. Then I then met the president of Proliant and

Figure 6-1. Skeleton model of the transfer process.

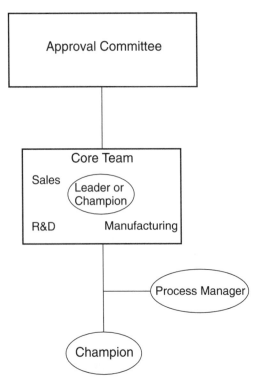

briefly discussed the importance of a formal new product transfer process. I met with the team for the rest of the day. The prepicked group numbered 15 from all areas of the company—both management and technical personnel from research, manufacturing, quality assurance, business sectors, human resources, and marketing. During our meeting, I used some of the techniques from Tool 5, Productive Meetings. The agenda had been preset and distributed to all members (see Figure 6-2).

Figure 6-2. Initial meeting agenda.

Meeting Agenda
January 9, 1998

10–11 A.M.	Introductions
	Review of model proposed
11–12 A.M.	Transfer process concept
12–1 P.M.	Lunch
1–2 P.M.	Buy-in to proceed
2–3 P.M.	Pick formal development team
3–4 P.M.	Review timing
4–5 P.M.	Modify model/path forward

During the meeting a formal development team was chosen to proceed with the development of the transfer process. All those in attendance recorded their own work preference profile, and from the results we chose six people to proceed as the development team. Figure 6-3 shows the six-person team, along with their profiles and work areas.

Figure 6-3. Development team profiles.

Name	Work Area	Profile
Member 1	Research and Development	ECAS
Member 2	Research and Development	ICAF
Member 3	Quality Assurance	EPBF
Member 4	Business Unit Manager	ECAS
Member 5	Manufacturing	IPBS
Member 6	Technical Sales	ICAF

The team was almost a perfect balance of work areas and work preferences. Research and development, manufacturing, sales, the business unit, and quality assurance (QA) were all represented. There was also a good balance of work preferences:

Extroverts	3
Introverts	3
Practical	2
Creative	4
Analytical	4
Beliefs	2
Structured	3
Flexible	3

Next, the group of 15 reviewed the timing for development and implementation of a formal process. This was more of a "wished-for" timing. It was decided that if we started immediately, a process could be rolled out to the organization by the beginning of summer, which would mean in about four months. Before the next meeting, the realities of a four-month schedule would have to be reviewed to see if the time frame was realistic.

Then we took a cut at the skeleton model. The group decided that the model addressed the major elements of a structure for the transfer process. They all agreed that the champion, who starts the process by initiating the first new product form, should be on top and that the approval committee should be on the bottom in more of an advisory capacity. Also, the feeling of the group was that QA and a business unit manager (BUM) should also be represented on the core team. The modified model looked like Figure 6-4.

Figure 6-4. Modified model of the transfer process.

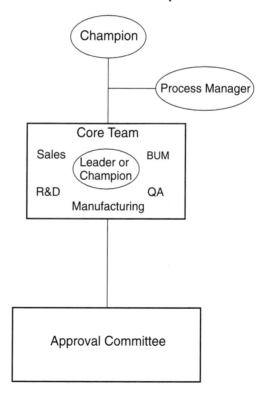

The team wanted to name the transfer process, so the whole organization could identify with a name. We came up with the acronym PRIDE:

PRoduct and

Idea

Development

Excellence

The group embraced this acronym and thought that a pride of lions could be the logo.

The next meeting of the development team was set for two days, January 22–23, 1998, to be held off-site.

January 22–23, 1998

In preparation for the meeting, Steve and I worked on a schedule for the development of the transfer process. The major work tasks were: develop the process model, present the model to management, prepare the PRIDE overview and users' guide, prepare the notebook, train the PRIDE manager, and implement the process. The schedule is shown in Figure 6-5.

If we stayed on schedule we would be able to get the work done by the beginning of summer.

The agenda for the two-day meeting is shown in Figure 6-6.

Figure 6-5. Process schedule.

Task \ Week of:	1/12	1/19	1/26	2/2	2/9	2/16	2/23	3/2	3/9	3/16	3/23	3/30	4/6	4/13	4/20	4/27	5/4	5/11	5/18	5/25	6/1	6/8	6/15	6/22
Develop Skeleton Model	xxxxxx																							
Prepare for Workshop																								
Two-Day Proliant Workshop			xx																					
Develop Model				xxxx																				
Present to Proliant Management, etc			xxxx																					
Modify Model and Process						xxxx																		
Prepare Products									xxxxxxxxxxxxxxxxxx															
PRIDE Overview																								
PRIDE User's Guide																								
Notebook Prep. and Edit											xxxxxxx													
Notebook Printing													xxxxxxx											
Train PRIDE Manager										xxxxxxxxxxxxxxxxx														
Proliant Training—3 Days														xxxx										
Facilitate 1st PRIDE Implementation																								
Spot Consult (Beyond 1st Implementation)																xxxxxxxxxxxxxxxxxxxxxxxxxxx								

DMB:br
1/12/1998

Figure 6-6. Development team agenda.

Product and Idea Development Excellence Workshop
January 22–23, 1998

Thursday:

Revisit model
Set up team objectives (using SMART)
Review transfer tools and pick which ones are applicable

Review current forms/reports/templates
Establish deliverables chart

Friday:

Continue with deliverables chart
Skeleton of Stage-Gate

Set up PRIDE metrics
Prepare for management review

Path forward

REVISIT THE TRANSFER MODEL

The first topic on the agenda was to revisit the transfer model. In structure, it was agreed to, but the team wanted to incorporate four additions:

1. Use existing approval forms as a guide during the process.

2. Show the interface of work teams reporting to the core team.

3. Show that the customer and supplier are integrated into the model.

4. Include three directors on the Approval Committee.

The revised model now looked as shown in Figure 6-7.

Figure 6-7. Revised model of the transfer process:
The PRIDE process model.

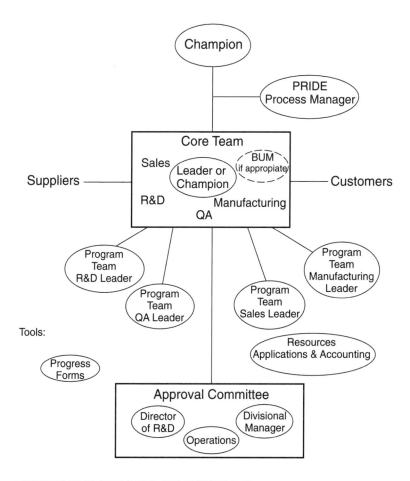

ESTABLISH SMART OBJECTIVES

The team next began charting objectives for the PRIDE process. There were eight goals for the process:

1. Reduce the cycle time of new ideas to market.

2. Increase the probability of project success.

3. Develop more products and ideas companywide.

4. Have management embrace PRIDE.

5. Be user friendly.

6. Develop market recognition.

7. Help to prioritize work.

8. Increase shareholder value.

These goals were put into a SMART objective, as shown in Figure 6-8.

Figure 6-8. SMART objectives.

S: PRIDE will be a formal transfer process that will accomplish eight corporate goals.

M: Metrics will be used to judge the success of the process.

A: This process will increase the shareholders' value and be embraced by upper management and employees.

R: The process is needed to be the "Best of the Best."

T: It will be developed and rolled out to the company by midsummer 1998.

REVIEW AND SELECT TRANSFER TOOLS

The 16 communications, task, and financial tools were then reviewed, and the team chose 10 of the 16 to try to incorporate in the formal transfer process as it was being developed:

Tool 1: SMART Objectives

Tool 3: Selecting a Cross-Functional Team

Tool 4: The Concept of a Champion

Tool 5: Productive Meetings

Tool 6: Fit-for-Use/Deliverables Checklist

Tool 10: Front-End Loading

Tool 11: Stage-Gate Methodology

Tool 12: Process Metrics

Tool 13: Process Audit

Tool 15: Economic Measures of Merit

REVIEW FORMS

We then discussed the six existing forms used and sign-offs required as a new product was being developed:

New Idea Form

Bench Test Worksheet

Pilot Test Worksheet

Request for Plant Test

Product Formula Form

Request for Product Label Change

Each form had places for at least 12 signatures, and typically the company was not very successful in having the forms signed. Nevertheless, the team felt that the forms could be modified to include less information and fewer required signatures. With these changes, the forms could become a vital part of the transfer process.

ESTABLISH THE DELIVERABLES CHART

To begin putting together a Stage-Gate process, the heart of a successful transfer process, it is imperative to make a checklist of all the deliverables that are necessary for a successful product launch. The team began this exercise by charting all tasks they felt were important to the transfer process. The list of tasks is shown in Figure 6-9.

IDENTIFY THE STAGE-GATE PROCESS

The teams then broke into small groups and listed the common stages that the majority of Proliant projects go through. The team members then reconvened, and a consensus of the common stages was put together. There was only a small amount of discussion of these stages because most team members had come up with the identical stages:

- Idea concept

- Bench tests

- Pilot plant tests

- Plant tests

- Construction

- Implementation

Figure 6-9. Tasks important to the transfer process.

Internal product alpha testing
External product beta testing
Idea discussion (champion)
Back-of-the-envelope calculations
Identifying core team
Formulas, process procedures, and standard operating procedures
Final product specifications
Finalizing and constructing facility
Process debugging
Value of positioning with the customer
Initial product specifications
Market launch
Facility concept
QA/regulatory requirements
Idea/product definition and optimization
Idea/product further optimization
Targeting market
Preliminary business plan
Business plan (first draft)
Business plan (finalized)
First production run
PRIDE metrics
Patent inquiry
Patent search
Refining idea/product concept
Auditing idea/product

These stages were adopted into the PRIDE process. I added two more stages—one in the beginning (Pre-PRIDE) and one at the end (Post-PRIDE). Therefore, the stages of the PRIDE process are:

■ Stage 0: Pre-PRIDE

■ Stage 1: Idea concept

■ Stage 2: Bench tests

■ Stage 3: Pilot plant tests

■ Stage 4: Plant tests

■ Stage 5: Construction

■ Stage 6: Implementation

■ Stage 7: Post-PRIDE

The team next organized the tasks or deliverables according to what stages had to be completed before proceeding to the next stage. Figure 6-10 shows the deliverables in the stages in which they occur.

DEVELOP PROCESS METRICS

To make sure that the PRIDE process would perform according to its objectives, the team developed metrics by which the process would be judged. They are listed in Figure 6-11.

At the conclusion of this two-day meeting, the PRIDE development team had unanimously agreed to the following:

■ The objective of the PRIDE transfer process was established.

Figure 6-10. PRIDE Stage-Gate methodology.

To process the following cases: new products or line extensions, applications, upgrade products/processes, new formulations, cost savings, and label changes.

Stage 0	Stage 1	Stage 2	Stage 3	Stage 4	Stage 5	Stage 6	Stage 7
Pre-PRIDE	Idea Concept	Bench Tests	Pilot Plant Tests	Plant Tests	Construction, Installation or Dismantling	Implementation	Post-PRIDE
Champion-Idea Discussion	Target Market						Audit Idea/Product
Back of the Envelope Economics	Preliminary Business Plan		Business Plan (first draft)	Business Plan (finalized)			
Initial Product Specifications	Refine Idea/Product Concept & Lab Samples	Idea/Product Definition And Optimization	Idea/Product Further Optimization	Formulas Process Procedures SOP's		First Production Run	
Value of Positioning w/Customer	Customer Liaison		Internal Product Alpha Testing	External Product Beta Testing		Market Launch	
Core Team Identified	Environmental Implications		QA/Regulatory Requirements Environmental	Final Product Specifications		Process Debugging	
	Patent Search		Facility Concept		Finalize and Construct Facility		
	Supplier Contact		Co-Packer Approval				PRIDE Metrics
GATES: ◇	◇	◇	◇	◇	⊙	⊙	◇
CYCLE TIME (months)							

Stage 0 Forms:	Stage 1 Forms:	Stage 2 Forms:	Stage 3 Forms:	Stage 4 Forms:			
(1) - New Idea Form	(3) - Business Plan	(4) - Bench and Pilot Worksheet	(4) - Bench and Pilot Worksheet	(5) - Request for Pilot and Plant Test		◇	Approval Committee Review
(2) - Request for Ingredients				(6) - Co-Packer Approval		⊙	Steering Committee Review
				(7) - Product Formula			
				(8) - Request for Product Label			

Figure 6-11. PRIDE metrics.

Percent of projects with customer involvement

Definition:
There are six specific tasks throughout the PRIDE process methodology that refer to involving the customer. Is this occurring?

Number of PRIDE references out of Proliant, Inc.

Definition:
The number of times the core team hears the PRIDE process mentioned by suppliers and/or customers during the development process.

PR campaign that will highlight PRIDE

Definition:
Does the sales literature used during market launch mention the value of using the PRIDE process?

Are progress forms being used?

Definition:
How many of the eight forms have been filled out and kept on record by the PRIDE process manager?

Actual versus forecast cycle times

Definition:
Months required to move from Stage 0 to completion of Stage 6, and months required to complete each stage versus forecast. The forecast number will be reviewed by the PRIDE process manager for consistency.

Actual versus forecast shareholders' value

Definition:
Percent increase in Return on Equity (ROE) versus the amount forecast.

Tally sheet

Definition:
A list of all PRIDE projects.

Number of projects through gates

Definition:
Total number of interim Gate reviews held during a project.

Number of successful projects

Definition:
Total number of PRIDE projects completed versus the total number started.

Number of projects through Stage 3

Definition:
Total number of Gate 4 reviews.

- The champion would initiate the process by submitting a concept form to the PRIDE process manager.

- A core team from R&D, Manufacturing, QA, and Marketing would be formed for each project using the personnel preference system.

- The approval team would be composed of the first-line supervision from each department on the core team.

- Generic PRIDE stages were established for all projects.

- Deliverable tasks were set out.

- A process development timetable was established.

- The PRIDE metrics were agreed to.

As a path forward, we decided to begin developing a notebook to document the PRIDE process and prepare for presenting our plan to upper management for approval at the next meeting. The next meeting was set for February 19–20.

February 19–20, 1998

The development team had fleshed out all the elements of the PRIDE process. At the scheduled management review meeting on February 19, the team reviewed the total process. Management only had one suggestion: that before proceeding to Stage 4, a project core team would get approval to proceed by upper management if the capital expenditure for the project was expected to exceed $100 million. Overall, they were very pleased with the process and gave us their support.

A first cut of the PRIDE manual was reviewed February 20 and modified. It was agreed that a cost-estimating and cash flow spreadsheet to guide each core team's project economics was needed.

The development team felt that it would take one month to complete the notebook, and a review meeting was set for March 12.

March 12–13, 1998

The development team completed the PRIDE process notebook (see the Appendix) and decided to review it with the R&D organization to gain its buy-in. We also wanted Marketing to review the process so it could begin thinking about how to launch the PRIDE process to the Proliant organization and its customers. Our next meeting was scheduled for April 2.

April 2–3, 1998

In three separate meetings, the PRIDE development team reviewed the proposed process with the R&D organization. At each meeting, we solicited comments and changes designed to improve the process. After the meetings, the development team reviewed all the comments and decided on the changes to incorporate. These changes were reviewed with the R&D organization so we felt we had buy-in to proceed with launching the process.

To launch the PRIDE process, the Marketing group proposed the following items:

- A bulletin describing the PRIDE process would be placed on each bulletin board, signed by the development team and the president.

- Everyone would be given a PRIDE T-shirt.

- All employees would attend scheduled training.

- A monthly newsletter would be issued summarizing all projects going through the PRIDE process.

- A large banner announcing PRIDE would be draped over the facilities entrance.

- Everyone would receive a PRIDE process PC screen saver.

The development team agreed with these launch strategies. We planned to train the Proliant organization and launch the PRIDE process the week of April 28.

Week of April 28, 1998

In four-hour meetings held throughout the week, over 200 employees were trained in the PRIDE process.

The development team agreed to meet at the end of May to review current projects just entering the process and discuss with the teams their impressions and comments on the new process.

May 27–28, 1998

Five projects were going through the PRIDE process. Each project champion and core team met with the development team to review their status. The PRIDE process was working well, and it was deemed a success.

One Year Later

The PRIDE process has been embraced by the whole organization. The first year's metrics show that the objectives of the process are being met. Proliant had begun a champion and core team compensation program, which has since spread to a companywide compensation program. All new employees are trained in the PRIDE process as part of their orientation. The PRIDE process is successfully transferring new products from R&D through manufacturing to product launch. The cycle time of the 50 projects that have gone through the process has been reduced by approximately 50 percent.

Epilogue

The information in this book comes from successful methods that have become practice. Over the years that I have been consulting on this subject, many companies have implemented a successful transfer process based on this information. Transferring new products successfully from R&D through manufacturing and product launch is a common problem throughout industry. Although there is great potential for success, there are two problems that companies typically struggle with.

First, and most important, the transfer process, just like a new product, needs a champion inside the company. This must be an individual who has a passion and sees the need for and benefits of such a process, like Steve Welch from Proliant. He saw a great need for a transfer process because his success in his new job as the vice president of R&D directly related to the number of successful new products that came out of his department and were implemented by the corporation. As a consultant, I can only teach, recommend, and guide. A true champion within a corporation will be the driver to make sure the project is a success. After reading this book, you or one of your colleagues might be that champion.

Second, the degree of upper management support for this process can make it or break it. A well-developed transfer process will require resources—both dollars and people. Management must recognize the need for the transfer process and be willing to commit to its successful implementation.

Everything else may be discussed, developed, modified, and made to work when the journey toward a new product transfer process has a champion and upper management support.

A successful transfer process will give your company the competitive edge it needs to stay ahead and stay profitable. The goal of any business is to make money. Statistics show that 45 percent of all revenues comes from new products. The success rate of these new products will be affected positively by a structured methodology that the whole company uses.

This book has presented two phases for a successful transfer process: using and incorporating proven tools and techniques into the process and developing and implementing a process that will have buy-in from the whole corporation.

Proliant's Transfer Process Notebook

Proliant PRIDE Process User Guide

5A. Stage-Gate Methodology

A Stage-Gate Methodology

Structure Hierarchy

Stage-Gate Overview

Stage Summaries

Cycle Time Guide

5B. Gate Reviews

Definition

Purpose

Decisions

Before a Gate Review

Presentation Standards

6. Approval Committee

Overview

Responsibilities

Approval Committee Deliverables

AC Gate Reviews: Meeting Ground Rules

Results

7. Customer/Supplier Interface

Definition

Stage-Gate

8. PRIDE Metrics

PRIDE Goals

Use of Metrics

9. Financial Valuation

Purpose

Responsibility

Templates

10. Eight Proliant Progress Forms [These forms are not shown for security reasons.]

1. INTRODUCTION

What Is PRIDE?
PRIDE:

- Is an acronym that stands for **PR**oduct and **I**dea **D**evelopment **E**xcellence.

- Is a process that provides Proliant, Inc. with a structured methodology for new product/idea development through successful implementation that will:

  Yield faster cycle times

  Lower development costs

  Increase the probability of project successes

Provide a sharper focus on the marketplace

Yield robust new offerings

Increase overall communications within Proliant, Inc.

- Is a user-friendly process tied into Proliant, Inc.'s strategic business plan that will ultimately increase shareholder value.

- Is applied to a myriad of development activities within Proliant, Inc., including applications, new formulations, new products or processes, cost saving programs, and label changes.

- Is fully supported by management and part of Proliant, Inc. culture.

- Is structured to increase organizational responsibility for new ideas and products.

- Is structured to increase front-end efforts.

PRIDE Development Team

Members:

[Member 1]	R&D
[Member 2]	Business
[Member 3]	Business
[Member 4]	Sales
[Member 5]	Business
[Member 6]	Quality Assurance
[Member 7]	Manufacturing
[Member 8]	Administrative Support

[Member 9] (Adviser)   R&D
[Member 10] (Consultant)

What Are the Elements of PRIDE?

The following chart and diagram [Figure A-1] illustrate the eight key elements of PRIDE and show how they support the PRIDE Process [Figure A-2].

Element	Description
Champion	The passionate originator of the new idea or product
Core Team	The developers and leaders, supported by many program teams
PRIDE Process Manager	Resource who facilitates, trains, coaches, and advises the Core Team and maintains PRIDE within the organization
Approval Committee	The decision makers
Customer/Supplier	Market focus resources
Stage-Gate Process	A common structured methodology shared among programs
Gate Reviews	Scheduled at milestones; the decision point for the Process—dollars and resources
Progress Forms	Proliant, Inc.'s eight progress forms

Figure A-1. PRIDE Process model.

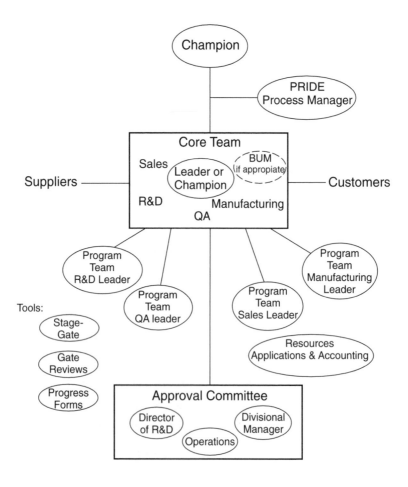

Figure A-2. PRIDE Stage-Gate Process.

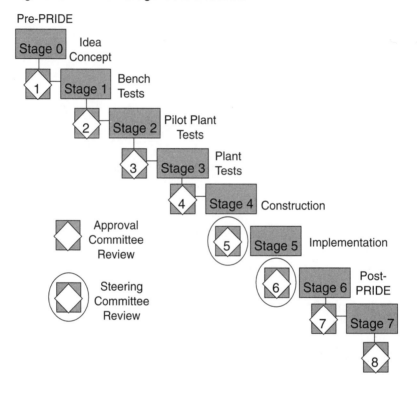

2. CHAMPION

Overview

The Champion begins the whole PRIDE Process by initiating the Idea Form.

This form may be filled out by anyone within Proliant, Inc. A new product or idea should be carefully thought out before an Idea Form is filled out.

A Champion is someone who:

- is passionate about the product or idea

- has a clear vision

- wants to succeed beyond all

- feels accountable

Roles and Responsibilities of the Champion

- Initiates the New Idea Form

- Works with the PRIDE manager to evaluate the proposal and to evaluate the strategic importance and business merit of the product or idea

- Chooses the Core Team members who will work with the Champion throughout the PRIDE Process

- Prepares the back-of-the-envelope economic calculation

- Is responsible that the Business Plan be developed throughout the Process

- Presents the product or ideas at the Gate 1 Review

- Keeps the purpose, goals, and approach relevant throughout the PRIDE Process

- Is an active participant in the Core Team

- Provides "vision" in Core Team meetings and Gate Reviews

- Acts as a formal liaison for the Core Team, PRIDE Process Manager, and Approval Committee between Gate Reviews

3. PRIDE PROCESS MANAGER

The management and continuous improvement of the PRIDE Process are led by the PRIDE Process Manager who:

- Helps Core Team use PRIDE (assists in organizing and planning projects and in preparation of Gate Reviews).

- Reports to Approval Committee.

- Trains and interprets the methodology for the organization.

- Maintains records, collects and reports on PRIDE Metrics.

Roles and Responsibilities

Helps Core Team Use the PRIDE Process

- Participates with Core Team (facilitates)
- Helps to set direction of Stage-Gate path
- Monitors team progress
- Resource to Champion
- Facilitates resource commitments
- Participates in audit of project

Reports to Approval Committee

- Coordinates Gate Reviews
- Records minutes at all Gate Review meetings
- Shares PRIDE Metrics (continuous improvement)
- Notifies Divisional Managers/Approval Committee of potential stoppers

Trains the Organization

- Maintains training materials
- Conducts training for new Core Team members
- Prepares PRIDE newsletter (bulletin board)
- Trains project management skills and financials

Maintains Records

- Ensures all eight forms are completed

- Keeper of the project records (central file)

- Updates the PRIDE Process when necessary

- Maintains the metrics database

- Maintains the PRIDE User Guide

- Maintains Proliant personal profiles

4. CORE TEAM

- A single Core Team is formed for each PRIDE project.

- Members may be assigned full- or part-time depending on the project needs and stage of development.

- Members are assigned for the duration of the project; however, necessary team member transitions are managed through the Gate Review process. Gate Reviews are held before beginning the next stage.

- The Champion is the initial leader; however, other leaders may evolve as the project progresses through the stages.

- The Core Team will include members from cross-functional areas: Research and Development (R&D), Quality Assurance (QA), Sales, and Manufacturing. If appropriate a Business Unit Manager (BUM) may also be a member of the Core Team. Team size should be determined at the Gate 1 Review; however, it should never be more than six people.

■ Each Core Team member has a defined role and a set of responsibilities.

■ The Core Team manages the project through the stages. The Core Team will meet on an as-needed basis. Meetings will be scheduled by the current leader.

Core Team Definition

The Core Team is a cross-functional team originally chosen by the Champion. The Champion reviews his or her choices for the team with the PRIDE Process Manager and makes modifications accordingly. Core Team members' availability will be cleared through the Departmental Manager. The team is then chartered by the Approval Committee at the Gate 1 Review and will stay together throughout the project. Necessary personnel changes may be managed through that review process.

This Team has the responsibility to manage the project from conceptualization through commercialization and the project audit. The Team has the authority, personnel, and resources allocated by the Approval Committee to accomplish the tasks in any particular stage. All project responsibilities associated with organizing, planning, and coordinating the project's efforts are divided among the team members. The Core Team members represent R&D, QA, Sales, and Manufacturing. If appropriate a Business Unit Manager (BUM) may also be a member of the Core Team. The BUM would work closely with the PRIDE Process

Manager and the Champion to ensure project excellence in his or her area and proper strategic business fit.

For small projects, Core Team members may represent more than their own area. For larger projects, each Core Team member will represent his or her own area. For the few very large projects, the PRIDE Process Manager may suggest more than one member from a functional area be represented on the Core Team.

The Core Team is asked to: make decisions during the stages, coordinate and plan concurrent activities, and recommend strategic direction at the Gate Reviews. This will ensure that correct decisions are made early in the development cycle, avoiding costly changes later.

Members must realize that to be chosen to participate on a Core Team is an honor, and they must respect other members and value their opinions. Members must also recognize the principle that each individual is only as successful as the team.

The Core Team will designate a member to be the key contact with suppliers. The Sales Core Team member will be the key contact with the customers. It is up to the Core Team to communicate with suppliers and customers and invite them to participate in key meetings.

Project Teams

Individual Core Team members will lead a Project Team from their specific area. Members should work with the Divisional or Departmental Manager to ensure Project Team members' availability. Core Team members are the key communicators with the people in their functional areas. The Project Team member's participation will be dis-

cussed at the Gate Reviews. Employees assigned to a
Project Team will be responsible for a specific task within
a stage, but will not be responsible for overall project planning, decisions, or project coordination. Their progress will
be communicated to other Core Team members by the
Project Leader. The Core Team Leader will select the
Project Team members based on expertise, interpersonal
skills, and existing relationships.

Project Team members are assigned to the project until
the tasks are completed. Members may or may not be
involved with the Team throughout the project.

Support personnel or resources, especially in the areas
of Applications and Accounting, will be asked to work
with the Project Teams when appropriate. They will usually be responsible for a subset of tasks or activities within
a stage. The Team Leader will coordinate their work with
the Project Team. Should this be an unusually large effort,
the Project Team Leader will get approval for prolonged
participation from the Departmental Manager.

5A. STAGE-GATE METHODOLOGY

Overview

- The methodology is composed of stages and tasks
  as a generic starting framework for Core Teams.

- Divided into stages marking key milestones for
  strategic decisions.

- Further specified into tasks of execution and cross-
  functional coordination:

R&D

Manufacturing

Sales

QA

- Tailored by the Core Team to meet specific needs of a particular project.

- Used as a road map for new products or line extensions, applications, upgrade of products/processes, new formulations, cost-saving projects, and label changes.

A Stage-Gate Methodology

"A game plan for product innovation is one solution to what ails so many firms' new product projects. Facing increasing pressure to reduce the cycle time yet improve their new product success rates, companies are increasingly looking to new product game plans, or 'Stage-Gate systems,' to manage, direct, and control their product-innovation efforts. That is, they have developed a systematic process—a blueprint or road map—for moving a new product through the various stages and steps from idea to launch. Game plans work! Begin the design of this game plan with a quick look at what this new product process must achieve. Six goals of a new product game plan would be: quality of execution, sharper focus and better prioritization, fast-paced parallel processing, a multi-functional team approach, a strong market orientation, and better homework up-front."[1]

A structured, consistent approach to development helps

an organization rapidly initiate an effort and drive to a logical end point through a series of stages and gates. This approach increases efficiency and reduces cycle time by "standardizing" repeatable stages and tasks from one project to the next, and through the audit of the process allows individuals to learn from the experiences of previous projects that have gone through the Stage-Gate Process. Some benefits of a structured Stage-Gate Process are:

- Consistent methodology tailored to the needs of an individual project.

- Common understanding of the stages and tasks within each stage, implementation procedures, and responsibilities.

- More effective teamwork across functional lines.

- Problem resolution early in the life of the process.

- Improved communication.

Structure Hierarchy

Every development project will go through a series of stages, each of which represents a major segment of the overall process. After completion of a current stage, before passing through to the next stage, a review will be held where major project decisions will be made either to go on to the tasks in the next stage, redirect efforts within the current stage, or stop all efforts on the project. The stages are further divided into major tasks that fulfill the requirement of the stage. The PRIDE Process Manager will define the stages and tasks that each Core Team should consider.

The specific activities associated with each task are not defined but left for the Core and Project Teams to define based on the unique needs of each project.

Stage Summaries

Stage 0: Pre-PRIDE

The Champion begins by filling out a **New Idea Form**. He or she then reviews this with the PRIDE Process Manager, who along with the appropriate Divisional Manager or designate (i.e., Business Unit Manager) assesses the strategic fit, business merit, and technical feasibility of the new idea.

If warranted, the Champion begins to explore alternative technical solutions and begins to put together initial project specifications along with back-of-the-envelope economics. Back-of-the-envelope economics will be discussed in the Financial Valuation section.

The Champion chooses his or her own Core Team members. These members are reviewed with the PRIDE Process Manager, and any modifications to the team are made. The sales member of the Core Team immediately assesses the value of positioning this new idea with the customer. The Core Team begins to work on this new idea, clarifying the technology and its value, in preparation to a Gate 1 Review to be held with the Approval Committee. Stage 0 tasks are less complex than those of subsequent stages, and there are more assumptions and uncertainties. Estimates of technology, alternatives, product costs, development requirements, and market potential, however, are sufficient for the Approval Committee to decide on the new idea's future.

Stage 1: Idea Concept

In this stage the idea or product concept is refined and the target market identified. Estimates of market and business opportunity, technical feasibility, and personnel required for the development are solidified and the skeleton of the **Business Plan** is begun.

Financial sensitivity analysis is done to determine the focus of additional studies. Focus is still on meeting the customer's needs and beginning interfacing with various customers, but the study is broadened to include the availability of suppliers for the essential materials. The idea's competitive position is studied and a patent inquiry made.

The Core Team prepares the necessary information for a review with the Approval Committee at Gate 2. Also at this point in the development cycle, if it appears likely this project will require sizable funding to commercialize, it would be prudent to plan to review the project at a regularly scheduled monthly Steering Committee meeting.

Stage 2: Bench Tests

Product lab samples are made and the product definition and optimization at the bench scale completed; also, with the data collected an assessment of patentability is made. The Core Team will fill out the appropriate steps in the **Bench and Pilot Plant Worksheet.**

Toward the conclusion of Stage 2 the Core Team will prepare to review its work with the Approval Committee at a Gate 3 Review in anticipation of proceeding to Stage 3.

Stage 3: Pilot Plant Tests

Pilot plant samples are made, and the product definition goes through further optimization. The product samples made are tested internally through alpha testing.

The Core Team begins the first draft of the **Business Plan**.

QA begins to investigate regulatory requirements.

If a facility is needed for the product or a change to the existing facility required, the facility concepts are started in Stage 3.

To run the pilot plant tests, the **Request for Pilot and Plant Tests** must be filled out and the appropriate steps on the **Bench and Pilot Worksheet** completed.

The **Co-Packer Approval Form** must be completed, if appropriate.

Toward the conclusion of Stage 3, after three successful replications, the Core Team will prepare to review its work with the Approval Committee at a Gate 4 Review in anticipation of proceeding to Stage 4.

The environmental impacts are assessed.

Stage 4: Plant Tests

Stage 4 is one of the most important stages. At the end of this stage the Core Team will be reviewing its progress with the Steering Committee in preparation for beginning the construction of the facility or finalization of the idea or identifying a Co-Packer before implementation. The stage is the culmination of all product testing.

In this stage the Core Team will finalize the business plan, formulas, process, procedures, and standard operating procedures. Product made during the plant test will be used for beta testing with the customer before the final product specifications are locked in.

Forms to be filled out during this phase are the: **Request for Pilot and Plant Test**, **Product Formulas,** and a **Request for Label Change**, if appropriate.

Toward the conclusion of Stage 4, after three successful replications, the Core Team will prepare to review its work with the Steering Committee at a Gate 5 Review in anticipation of proceeding to construction, if necessary, and product implementation beginning with Stage 5.

Stage 5: Construction

Stage 5 only has one task, the installation and construction or dismantling and rearranging of the existing facility. Because there could be substantial dollars associated with this stage, upon completion the Core Team will again review its work with the Steering Committee at a Gate 6 Review.

Stage 6: Implementation

During Stage 6 the first production run will occur and the process will be debugged.

The market launch will have been planned and executed.

At the end of this stage the Core Team will have brought an idea or product all the way from conception through commercialization.

The Gate 7 Review will be held with the Approval Committee.

Stage 7: Post-PRIDE

This is a very important stage for the continuous improvement of the PRIDE process and the success of Proliant, Inc. It is during this stage that the process is audited and the PRIDE Metrics tallied.

It is only after completion of this stage and a final report given to the Steering Committee at Gate 8 that the Core Team is disbanded.

Cycle Time Guide

From the very first Stage Review at Gate 1, the Core Team is responsible for developing an overall schedule for commercialization or implementation. To aid in these forecasts, target timetables for completing each task of the development process need to be estimated.

There are however, a wide variety of ideas and products within Proliant, Inc., and the development time to implementation will vary. It is the responsibility of the Core Team to make the best estimate it can of the cycle time for all appropriate tasks and have that information available at the Gate 1 Review with the Approval Committee. The cycle time for each stage will be the minimum number on a task and extend to the maximum task timing. Since this methodology allows for parallel task completions, the cycle time for a given stage will be a range. This range should be filled in on the Stage-Gate chart and used for reference throughout the process. The PRIDE Process Manager will be a great help to the Core Team when trying to estimate the stage cycle times.

5B. GATE REVIEWS

Definition

Gate Reviews are scheduled meetings occurring after the completion of all the tasks within a given stage. These meetings are with the Core Team and the Approval Committee or Steering Committee depending on the stage just being completed. The Approval Committee or Steering Committee decides to continue, redirect, or cancel the project.

- Gate Reviews are working meetings between the Core Team and either the Approval Committee (All Gates) or the Steering Committee (Gates 5 and 6).

- Occur at major milestones or at changes in strategic direction.

- Focus on market direction, business decisions, and resource allocation (both dollars and people) to advance the project through the next stage.

- Mark endpoints to make decisions, not to start discussions.

- Reveal strategic thinking behind decisions.

Purpose

Gate Reviews are the most critical element in the development Stage-Gate methodology. During the Gate Reviews, the Approval Committee and/or Steering Committee make strategic decisions, allocate personnel, provide physical and financial resources, and give direction and leadership to the Core Team. They provide:

- An effective mechanism for making major decisions on new products or ideas.

- A forum for the Approval and/or Steering Committee to define the responsibility of the Core Team and delegate sufficient authority for it to execute the tasks required to get through the next stage.

- The link between business strategies and the development project.

- Formal, structured checkpoints to monitor the schedule and progress toward the project objectives.

PRIDE complements the normal contacts that are important to conducting business. By establishing a formal mechanism for reviewing major decisions, Gate Reviews strengthen communications, improve the quality of decisions, and promote closer cooperation within the organization.

Gate Reviews differ from technical reviews by focusing on the projects' business and strategic issues. They are not intended to take the place of technical reviews, project status reviews, or management presentations. These will still be held when needed.

Decisions

At each Gate Review, the Approval or Steering Committee directs the project in one of three ways:

GO: The project continues to the next stage as planned.

REDIRECT: The project is held in a certain stage or must repeat a previous stage.

NO GO: The project is canceled and the Core Team is reassigned.

The following list could be the reason for making a decision to cancel a project:

- The project is not financially attractive,

- An external event has affected the overall business strategy, or

- Other more attractive projects require resources previously committed to other projects.

Before a Gate Review

Scheduling

The Core Team Champion contacts the PRIDE Process Manager when he or she feels that all tasks have been successfully completed in one stage and are ready to proceed to the next stage.

Length

As a guide, Gate Reviews should last only one hour (45 minutes for the presentation and 15 minutes for questions).

Attendance

Attendance is limited to the Core Team members, the Approval or Steering Committee, and the PRIDE Process Manager.

Supporting Documentation

The supporting forms must be submitted to the PRIDE Process Manager for distribution at least five business days in advance of the scheduled meeting date.

After the Review

The PRIDE Process Manager documents the discussion and decisions and publishes these to the participants as soon as possible following the Gate Review meeting. Core Team members are responsible to communicate with the project teams the results of the Gate Reviews. The PRIDE Process Manager will include pertinent information in the next issue of the PRIDE newsletter.

Presentation Standards

The presentation should summarize the overall project in sufficient detail for the Approval or Steering Committee to understand issues and alternatives and make sound business decisions.

To monitor progress, cost, and direction, each Gate Review should include information on:

Marketing

Project budget

Schedule

Financial projections

Critical performance measures

Work plan

Clear tasks for the next phase

A general outline to be used as a guide may be seen below:

Introduction and background

Major issues and risks

Decisions required

Results of the stage

Technical overview

Business overview

Manufacturing overview

Financial overview

Project schedule and costs

Staffing and physical resources required

Recommendation

6. APPROVAL COMMITTEE

Overview

The Approval Committee (AC) is the middle layer of a two-tier decision-making structure of the PRIDE process. The AC formally interacts with the Core Team during Gate Reviews. Although the Steering Committee (SC) is the top decision-making tier and is part of the Gate 5 and 6 Reviews, the major authority for the PRIDE process rests with the AC.

The AC clearly defines roles and responsibilities of Project Teams and Core Team members so that the work of the Core Team can be accomplished quickly and efficiently. There are three members of the AC: the Director of R&D, the Divisional Business Manager for the business that has major control of the PRIDE project, and the Operations member. The committee as a whole must have full authority to make decisions on project direction and allocate resources to approved development projects.

There can be no off-line decision-making process, since this would defeat the two-tier decision structure of PRIDE and increase cycle time.

The SC will be part of Gate 5 and 6 Reviews; however, it will have *no* authority in the PRIDE process.

The AC is a permanent organizational structure which:

- Provides strategic direction for the PRIDE portfolio of projects.

- Ensures projects fit with business objectives.

- Conducts a business-focused review for each individual project on a stage-by-stage basis.

- Assigns or approves resources.

- Resolves issues that are beyond the authority or responsibility of the Core Team.

- Provides support and guidance on objectives for the next stage.

The Proliant, Inc. Approval Committee is composed of those representatives required to make the best business decisions on process or product development. The membership will ensure that the development projects are consistent with the overall business strategy and receive the benefits of management expertise that is aware of all PRIDE projects throughout the organization. The AC is also responsible for feedback of all learnings shared by the Core Teams during a project audit to ensure continuous improvement and learning for new PRIDE projects.

Responsibilities

The AC, by making clear, coordinated decisions at the Gate Reviews, determines if the strategic direction and progress of the project:

- Justify a decision to continue the project into the next Stage ("Go"),

- Require substantive changes in strategy, definition, or objectives that will necessitate additional work in one or more steps of the current Stage ("Redirect"), or

■ Are sufficient for a decision to terminate the project, thus releasing resources for other projects ("No Go").

A project may be dropped because of insufficient progress or poor financial returns, or because there is a more attractive project requiring additional resources. Projects are terminated by the AC through the Gate Review mechanism for coordinated communications and effective reassignment of the Core and Project Team members.

The PRIDE Process Manager is responsible for scheduling meetings, issuing meeting minutes, and handling the general administrative details.

Approval Committee Deliverables

Those items that the AC is responsible for at each Gate Review are called AC deliverables. The AC deliverables are summarized below.

Gate 1 (after pre-PRIDE):

■ **Go, No Go, or Redirect**

■ *Approve* Core Team members or make suggestions for change

■ *Approve* project proposal

■ *Allocate* funding and people requirements for Stage 1

■ *Endorse* back-of-the-envelope economics

■ *Question* potential market

Gate 2 (after Idea Concept):

- **Go, No Go, or Redirect**
- *Approve* preliminary business plan
- *Scrutinize* financial sensitivities
- *Allocate* funding and people for Stage 2
- *Endorse* business opportunity
- *Question* supply chain needs
- *Scrutinize* environmental implications

Gate 3 (after Bench Tests):

- **Go, No Go, or Redirect**
- *Endorse* patentability
- *Allocate* funding and people for Stage 3
- *Confirm* marketability of product

Gate 4 (after Pilot Plant Tests):

- **Go, No Go, or Redirect**
- *Approve* first draft of business plan
- *Confirm* positive alpha testing
- *Approve* facility concept

- *Approve* funding and people for Stage 4

- *Endorse* regulatory requirements

- *Approve* Co-Packer if appropriate

- *Endorse* plan to deal with environmental issues

Gate 5 (after Plant Test):

- **Go, No Go, or Redirect**

- *Approve* final business plan

- *Endorse* final product/process

- *Allocate* funding and people for Stage 5

- *Confirm* positive product beta testing

Gate 6 (Construction):

- **Go, No Go, or Redirect**

- *Allocate* funding and people for Stage 6

Gate 7 (Implementation):

- **Go, No Go, or Redirect**

- *Confirm* successful product launch

- *Confirm* successful start-up

- *Reassign* personnel

Gate 8 (Post-PRIDE):

- Approve and record PRIDE Metrics

AC Gate Reviews: Meeting Ground Rules

All AC members *must make every effort to attend* all Gate Review meetings.

- No substitutes or proxies.

- Meeting will last no more than 60 minutes (starting and stopping on time).

- Quorum will be two out of three members.

- AC members who know in advance they will miss a meeting should notify the other AC members and give their perspective on any topic. It is the missing members' responsibility to catch up with any AC decisions made at the meeting.

Results

Through the Gate Review process the AC manages the entire development pipeline to allocate resources among active projects. Effective prioritizing of these projects and termination of less attractive projects are crucial elements for the success of Proliant, Inc.

7. CUSTOMER/SUPPLIER INTERFACE

Definition

"Working with suppliers to create unique value adds them to a firm's distinct competitive resources.

"Companies have long recognized that success requires getting close to the customer: Only by better serving the customer needs can firms outflank their rivals.

"Every firm is both a customer and a supplier. It is inconsistent to seek closer ties with one's customers while refusing to build the same kind of relationship with one's suppliers."[2]

Close collaboration between Proliant, Inc. and its suppliers and customers can produce dramatic results:

Higher Margins

Lower Costs

More Value for Customers

Larger Market Share

Reduced Cycle Time

Quality Improvements

Higher Probability of Success

Development of More Products Companywide

Stage-Gate

Early connections with both the customer and the supplier are a must with Proliant, Inc.'s PRIDE Stage-Gate Process. The Core Team will designate a member to be the key contact with any needed suppliers. The Sales Core Team member will be the key contact with the customers. It is up to the Core Team to make the necessary communication and invite the suppliers and customers to key meetings when necessary.

Stage 0: The customer is contacted to make sure the product or idea has a perceived value in the marketplace.

Stage 1: The target market is defined.

The supplier is contacted to ensure essential material flow and availability. Also preliminary prices are discussed.

Stage 2: Customer evaluation continues.

Stage 3: Customer evaluation continues.

Stage 4: External beta testing with the customer happens. Any changes or comments are fed back into the Core Team for action.

Stage 6: Once the product/process or idea is implemented, the customer satisfaction is gauged and corrections made.

8. PRIDE METRICS

PRIDE Metrics are used to monitor the PRIDE methodology and its effectiveness in creating positive change in the development activities. They also provide diagnoses of deficiencies in the PRIDE methodology and accelerate the adoption of new learnings in a continuous improvement mode. The PRIDE Process Manager maintains the metrics for the PRIDE Process. However, the Core Team is responsible for PRIDE Metrics for their project. Metrics are used during Gate Reviews when appropriate. The metrics are developed by the PRIDE Development Team and are based as measures of the effectiveness in accomplishing the goals.

PRIDE Goals

Reduce Cycle Time

Increase Probability of Success of Projects

Develop More Products and Ideas Companywide

Management Commitment to PRIDE Process

User Friendly

Market Recognition

Prioritization of Work

Increased Shareholder Value

The ten metrics are:

Percent of projects with customer involvement

Definition: There are six specific tasks throughout the PRIDE Process methodology that refer to involving the customer. Is this occurring?

Purpose: In order to be market-focused and continue to be throughout the process, making sure the final product meets the needs of the customer.

Number of PRIDE references out of Proliant, Inc.

Definition: The number of times the Core Team hears the PRIDE Process mentioned by suppliers and/or customers during the development process.

Purpose: To make sure that the suppliers and/or customers recognize that Proliant, Inc. is utilizing a development process that is focused on supplier/customer involvement and that the final product should meet the needs of the customer. This metric will show the value of using the PRIDE Process in the marketplace.

PR campaign that will highlight PRIDE

Definition: Does the sales literature used during market launch mention the value of using the PRIDE Process?

Purpose: To show the marketplace that Proliant, Inc. is focused on meeting the needs of the customer.

Are Progress Forms being used?

Definition: How many of the eight forms have been filled out and kept on record by the PRIDE Process Manager.

Purpose: The eight forms were written to document all the necessary information about the project so that a permanent record is maintained.

Actual versus forecast cycle times

Definition: Months required to move from Stage 0 to completion of Stage 6, and months required to complete each stage versus forecast. The forecast number will be reviewed by the PRIDE Process Manager for consistency.

Purpose: To build a database to determine how actual cycle time performance compares to expectations or external benchmarks. To increase the awareness of cycle time as an important indicator of success. Special attention should be paid not only to noting the actual cycle times, but also to relating the cycle times to factors such as team experience, project urgency, project delays, and project complexity.

Actual versus forecast shareholders' value

Definition: Percent increase in Return on Equity (ROE) versus the amount forecast.

Purpose: To determine the economic value of using the PRIDE Process.

Tally sheet

Definition: A list of all PRIDE projects.

Purpose: To monitor the use and effectiveness of PRIDE.

Number of projects through Gates

Definition: Total number of interim Gate Reviews held during a project.

Purpose: To monitor the Core Team's ability to meet Gate Review objectives as scheduled and proceed through the next stage.

Number of successful projects

Definition: Total number of PRIDE projects completed versus the total number started.

Purpose: To determine the number of successful projects.

Number of projects through Stage 3

Definition: Total number of Gate 4 Reviews.

Purpose: The PRIDE Process should do a good job of weeding out projects. This metric will note the number that proceed through to a plant test versus the total number started.

9. FINANCIAL VALUATION

Purpose

Financial estimates of the value/cost of the project are critical elements in the decision to launch the effort or to continue development. Financial estimates are used to:

- Estimate the economic benefits to the business (discounted cash flow and cost analysis).

- Compare attractiveness of projects to assign priority and allocate resources.

- Identify those areas which have the greatest economic benefit (sensitivity analysis).

- Determine the economic impact associated with specific uncertainties.

- Compare options within a project and select the most attractive one.

A working financial model (spreadsheet) is absolutely essential from the inception of a project, even though inputs to the model at the time are quite crude. As the project advances, inputs are redefined to eventually provide, at the time of commercialization, an accurate, detailed, and complete financial model incorporated in the final Business Plan of the new process or product.

Responsibility

The Champion is responsible for the development of the Business Plan and the overall financial model and for communicating its results. Other Core Team members are responsible for the data most closely associated with their functional areas:

Core Team Member	Financial Data
Sales	Sales Volume
	Selling Price
Manufacturing	Number of Operators
	Plant Operations
	Total Investment
	Process Yield
R&D	Materials
	—Unit Quantities
	—Prices

Templates

There will be two financial templates used within the PRIDE Process. The first template, titled **Proliant— Financial Template for Stage 0**, will be used within Stage 0 to estimate back-of-the-envelope economics. It may be seen on the following page [omitted]. This template was constructed to allow the Core Team to establish an estimate of the total costs of the product and the Net Present Value (NPV). The NPV is an economic measure of merit that quantifies the magnitude of the financial impact to the business. If the NPV is positive, it means that the project will earn the cost of capital[3] on the investment made plus an additional amount. There are only six key inputs of data and they are indicated on the template by the colored shaded areas. These inputs are: number of operators, plant operations, material price, process yield, sales volume, total investment, and average selling price. When these data are entered, the spreadsheet will automatically calculate the Total Costs and NPV.

The second template, titled **Proliant—Financial Template for Stage 1**, will be used within Stage 1 to calculate the NPVs for various key uncertain variables. (This spreadsheet may be seen two pages back [omitted].) Sensitivity analysis will be the output of this template and will provide important information on the financial impact of the variables. The sensitivity analysis is framed in the context of probabilities of future outcomes. For each input variable selected for the sensitivity analysis, the Core Team member estimates a range of 10% to 90% probability of occurrence. There are four key variables: sales volume, sales price, cash expenses, and investment. The Core Team member answers two questions for each variable:

- What is a value of cash expense so low or sales volume so high that there is a 10% chance it will happen?

- What is a value of cash expense so high or sales volume so low that there is a 90% chance it will happen?

NOTES

1. Robert G. Cooper, *Winning at New Products: Accelerating the Process from Idea to Launch, 3d Edition* (Reading, Mass.: Perseus Books, 2001).

2. Jordan D. Lewis, *The Connected Corporation* (New York: Simon & Schuster, 1995).

3. Proliant, Inc.'s weighted average cost of equity and cost of borrowing, which is used as the discount factor in the discounted cash flow analysis. The current cost of capital is 12%.

Index

activity, definition of, 52
administrative costs, 77–79
alpha testing, 174
alternatives, 45–48
approval, 137–138, 156
approval committee, 150(fig.)
   attendance rules, 176
   deliverables, 173–176
   organizational role, 171–172
   and resources, 156, 173
   responsibilities, 172–173
   role, 149, 161, 162, 164
approval forms, 131–132, 137
audit, of process, 56–59, 154
audit stage, 51
authority, 156, 171
automation, of testing, 44

bench tests, 50, 162–163, 174
beta testing, 164, 175, 178
Box-Behken, 43–44
brainstorming, 46–48, 98
Briggs Myers, Isabel, 21
business plan, 153, 162, 163, 174
business unit manager, 125

cancellation, 160, 168, 173
capital, cost of, 86–89

case studies
   cost estimation, 79
   cross-functional team, 24–26
   labor costs, 70–72
   material costs, 65–67
   prioritization, 91–92
   process audit, 57–58
   product transfer (Proliant), 119–142
   Stage-Gate method, 52–53
cash flow analysis, 82–85, 138
champion
   defined, 26, 149
   and financial model, 184
   functions, 152–153, 155, 161, 168
   and reviews, 168
   role, 20–21, 27, 95–96, 125, 137, 141
change, 95–96
   see also redirection
Co-Packer, 163, 175
coach, 149
collaboration, 19
commitment, 16, 20, 52
communication
   and cross-functional team approach, 19
   with customers, 31–32, 157, 162, 177–178, 180

187